IN MAREMMA

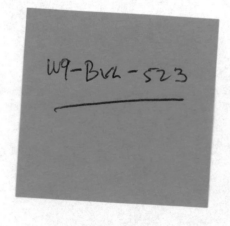

IN MAREMMA

Life and a House in Southern Tuscany

David Leavitt
and
Mark Mitchell

COUNTERPOINT
WASHINGTON, D.C.

Portions of this book have appeared in different form in
Food & Wine and *Travel & Leisure.*

Library of Congress Cataloging-in-Publication Data
Leavitt, David, 1961–
In Maremma : life and a house in southern Tuscany /
by David Leavitt and Mark Mitchell.
p. cm.
ISBN 1-58243-061-6 (alk. paper)
1. Maremma (Italy)—Description and travel.
2. Maremma (Italy)—Social life and customs.
3. Leavitt, David, 1961–. 4. Mitchell, Mark (Mark Lindsey)
I. Mitchell, Mark (Mark Lindsey) II. Title.
DG975.M43 L43 2001
940'.57—dc21   00-065862

FIRST PRINTING

Jacket and text design by David Bullen

Printed in the United States of America on acid-free paper
that meets the American National Standards Institute
z39–48 Standard.

COUNTERPOINT
P.O. Box 65793
Washington, D.C. 20035-5793

Counterpoint is a member of the Perseus Books Group

10 9 8 7 6 5 4 3 2 1

For Diane Mitchell

Contents

Traversando la Maremma Toscana

Dolce paese, onde portai conforme
l'abito fiero e lo sdegnoso canto
e il petto ov'odio e amor mai non s'addorme,
pur ti riveggo, e il cuor mi balza intanto.

Ben riconosco in te le usate forme
con gli occhi incerti fra 'l sorriso e il pianto,
e in quelle seguo de' miei sogni l'orme
erranti dietro il giovenile incanto.

Oh, quel che amai, quel che sognai, fu invano,
e sempre corsi, e mai non giunsi il fine:
e domani cadrò. Ma di lontano

pace dicono al cuor le tue colline
con le nebbie sfumanti e il verde piano
ridente ne le piogge mattutine.

Crossing the Tuscan Maremma

Sweet land, whence I derive
My habit of pride and my scornful song
And this bosom where hate and love are never appeased,
When I return to you, my heart leaps after so long.

I rediscover your familiar forms,
And through uncertain eyes, through smiles and tears,
Follow the errant tracks of dreams
That led to my youthful enchantment with you.

Oh, what I loved, what I dreamed was in vain,
After so much wandering, I never reached the end,
And tomorrow I'll die. But from afar

Your hills fill my heart with hope,
Steaming with mist and the green plains
Lovely in the morning rains.

Giosuè Carducci
Rime nuove XVI
(translated by Elena Giustarini)

IN MAREMMA

In Maremma

W E FIRST saw Podere Fiume, or River Farm, on a cold and rainy afternoon in January 1997. A plain, upright two-story house, it had been built in the 1950s as part of the Ente Maremma program to stimulate the economy of Southwestern Tuscany. No one had lived in it for more than twenty years. The downstairs consisted entirely of animal stalls, in the largest of which (the stall that would become our living room) there were stone troughs it would take three weeks to demolish. A crumbling outdoor staircase led to the apartment upstairs, which consisted of four rooms tiled in Necco wafer shades of terrazzo. In the big kitchen there was a Zappas wood-burning stove barely high enough for a child to cook at, an *echt*-fifties cabinet unit in yellow-and-blue Formica—this latter empty save for a drinking glass from a long-past promotion for Acqua Panna—and a carved stone sink.

Three doors opened off this kitchen. One led into a green bedroom with a reproduction of a Raphael Madonna hanging on the north wall, one into a pink bedroom that our poet friend

Henri Cole admonished us not to paint because it reminded him of Pompeii, and the third into a biscuit-colored bedroom that contained a rough straw bed and a stuffed egret. There was also a minute bathroom. No closets. Doves had built nests between the windows and the cypress-green shutters.

The house, as well as an outbuilding called a *porcellaio*—a shelter for pigs—sat on the crest *(poggio)* of a softly proportioned hill on about two acres of land, one of which was given over to forty olive trees and as many fruit trees: apricot, pear, nectarine, white peach, and three varieties of plum. At the base of the *poggio* a tree-lined little creek—dry during the summer months— curved alluringly. (It was because of this creek that the house had been named, a little grandly, Podere Fiume.) From upstairs one could see the hill where a famous battle had been fought in Roman times, the Monte Argentario peninsula, and the "sky-lines" of several villages: Saturnia, Montemerano, and Manciano. Around us there was gently sloping pastureland for sheep, as well as farmland that produced hay, wheat, and sunflowers, and a couple of small vineyards. The trees were mostly oaks, pines, and chestnuts. (One of the most beautiful, even moving sights we have here is that of a lone, gnarled, ancient oak in the middle of an expanse of green pasture.) There were few of the cypresses that are the presiding genius of the land around Florence, however, for the Maremmani associate them with cemeteries. Sheep, curled together for warmth on the hills, created the illusion of boulders cropping out from the grass.

An unexpected rhythm of this land is that it is green in the winter, when the days are short and one is needful of green, and parched brown in the summer, when the days are long, too long, and shutters have to be closed against the sun for hours. In a way, the land is like an actress: It always shows itself from its best angle.

WHEN WE were first living in Italy, the prospect of restoring a country house seemed so daunting to us as to be unthinkable. "The bureaucracy," we'd say whenever the subject came up. "Italian inefficiency," we'd say. And yet, perhaps because man and beast had lived peacefully together under its roof, Podere Fiume had a good soul (not to mention good bones); indeed, as we walked through it that first afternoon, the idea that we would bring the house back to life suddenly seemed natural, even inevitable. As it happened, the owner, a farmer and bon vivant with the extraordinary name of Loando, had had a stroke a few days earlier and was in the hospital in Pitigliano. With other houses we had looked at, the process of deciding whether to buy had been protracted, even tormented. That afternoon, however, something urged us to act impulsively, and we made an offer that, by the end of the day, Loando had accepted from his hospital bed. To our mild surprise, we jumped the bureaucratic hurdles gracefully, and on the first day of spring Podere Fiume legally became ours.

WE CAME to this part of Italy together for the first time in the autumn of 1993, partly because we wanted to flee Florence—so marvelous a city to visit and so taxing a city to live in—and partly because we wanted to "take" the famous thermal waters at Saturnia. These sulfury springs, which gush out of the earth at 37.5 degrees Celsius, were famous even in antiquity for their curative properties. On windy days the perfume of sulfur carries all the way up to the village, said to be the oldest in all of Italy. It was here that injured Roman soldiers were sent to be healed after battle. A hotel has now channeled the waters into a series of pools and artificial waterfalls, but they also flow down through an old and crumbling stone water mill to the natural falls known as the Cascate del Gorello.

The summer before we bought Podere Fiume, we thought about moving back to the United States, and looked at about eighty houses in Los Angeles and San Francisco—each of which turned out to have some fatal flaw: in earthquake-threatened San Francisco, a brick foundation; in Los Angeles, a power transformer in the backyard. The real flaw, of course, was in our hearts, which hankered for Tuscany. People assume that to live in Italy is necessarily more expensive than to live in America. This is and isn't true: Some things are more expensive, while others are less. But it is not money that makes a home, or lack of it that keeps one from being made. Podere Fiume spoke to us from its spirit, not its splendor. In Maremma, one does not find the vast and austere Tuscan villas that proliferate around Florence, Siena, and Lucca. Instead, houses tend to be on a modest scale and for the most part date only from the last century or two. Remains of the very oldest habitations in Italy, however—those of the Etruscans—are all around us.

ROUGHLY speaking, the Maremma corresponds to the province of Grosseto, which occupies the southwest corner of Tuscany. *Maremma* means "marsh," and for centuries this was exactly what the Maremma was. A few noble families had divided the land into a set of fiefdoms. The people were small in stature and accustomed to hardship. Women traveled on donkeyback; our neighbor Ilvo's younger sister, then only nine, was dragged to her death by a donkey whose rope she had tied around her waist to lead it by. Such accidents were common. This was the Wild West of Italy, home to the *butteri,* the Italian equivalent of cowboys, who tended herds of horned Maremmana cattle. (Seeing a horse tied in front of a bank or a bar is still not so unusual.) Even during the age of the Grand Tour, the threat of malaria dissuaded all but the most adventurous traveler from stopping here. Nor was the Maremma spared anything of Fascism or the Second World War. Bombs destroyed much of Grosseto, the principal city. Teracle, the real-estate agent under whose aegis we bought Podere Fiume (Magna Grecia names are common here), recalls witnessing, at thirteen, the shooting of an entire family by the blackshirts because they had given refuge for a few weeks to an English soldier. The father of our friend Brunella was beaten when he refused to sing the Fascist hymn at school.

Things started to change in the 1950s, when habitable land was claimed from the newly drained marshes and the threat of malaria eradicated. In addition, the government bought up most of the land from its feudal owners and distributed it among the tenant farmers whose families had been working it for generations. This program, the Ente Maremma, not only provided funding for hospitals and schools but put up houses for the farmers (Podere Fiume is one of these), more or less identical and cobbled together from stones and tufa, the porous volcanic rock also used by the Etruscans.

Today much of the Maremma is given over to an enormous national park. Wild boars, roebuck, and chamois abound in the forests; Maremmana sheepdogs—taciturn and tenaciously loyal, with thick, ivory-colored coats—guard huge flocks on many of the farms.* In contrast to Umbria, there is almost no industry: The people still make their living from agriculture. In the summer, when the afternoon temperature often reaches a hundred degrees, the farmers tractor by moonlight. Even after midnight we can hear the cool hum of their machines, watch the patient progress of these slow, majestic animals as they move over the fields.

What made the Maremma appealing to us—what made us want to live here far more than in one of the areas that foreigners had colonized (Chianti, or more recently, Umbria)—was that it still felt like a frontier. We did not know exactly what we would find here, only what we would not find: lovely, but in their efforts to be the "real" Italy, cartoon versions of hill towns (often ringed by factories); villages where it was possible almost never to hear Italian for all the English or German being spoken; the "snobbism of place" you become aware of when you overhear someone begin a sentence, "Of course, San Casciano dei Bagni was super-chic *last* year . . ." All of this seemed to us to defeat the point of living abroad: Although hiding in an enclave of one's countrymen is a way to be *in* a foreign land, it is not a way to be *part* of it. In Maremma, on the other hand, you could hear your own voice in the silence.

*A Maremmana also guards a flock of Persian carpets in a shop in Rome.

The House We Did Not Buy

AFTER WE decided that we wanted to live in Maremma, we looked at about twenty houses that were for sale. A restored Ente Maremma house, although lovely in a photograph, turned out, when we visited it, to stand only five feet from a new house its owner had just built for himself. Others were not houses at all, but halves of houses. In one case, though the half that was for sale had been carefully restored, with new plumbing and electricity and a glamorous kitchen, the other half resembled something out of an Erskine Caldwell novel. Finally we did see a house that we quite liked. It was one of a row of attached houses built in the thirties, in a tiny *borgo* just north of Montemerano. The owner was a Roman real-estate agent whose wife, an architect, had restored the small rooms with care, taking advantage of the house's high ceilings to install a loft-cum-sitting room in the bedroom, carving bathrooms out of thick walls, and adding a terrace on the roof. In the living room there was an enormous fireplace in front of which one could read on cold evenings, and out front a big garden with a grass lawn (rare in this part of the world where water is scarce), stone paths, roses, and an ancient oak tree.

After we saw the house, we pondered. In a certain sense, it fit our fantasies better than it did our needs. For example, it had only two bedrooms, which meant that one of us would have to do without a study and work in the living room or at the dining table. The living room was far too small ever to house the old upright Steinway Mark had inherited, and which we often spoke of moving from the States. There were no closets. And yet, and yet . . . the view from the terrace was so splendid, the kitchen had such attractive copper sinks and marble-tiled countertops, did it really matter if there weren't enough closets? After all, one didn't buy a house in Italy for the sake of storage space. Both our families had excesses of storage space, and what had they done with them? Stowed away boxes filled with creased sheets of wrapping paper, fondue sets, and televisions so old they actually had dials. This was not our style. Indeed, if anything, as we began our new life in Italy, we wanted to learn to edit our possessions more stringently: to own few things, but lovely things. What need had we of closets?

And so we paid another visit to the real-estate agent who had taken us to see the house (his name was Marco Rossi, which in Italy is like being named John Smith), expressed some timid interest, then inquired as to how we might proceed. He smiled and took a thickly stuffed file out of his desk. Because he liked to be completely up-front with his clients, he said, he wanted to make sure that we were aware from the beginning of certain "little problems" *(piccoli problemi)* with the house—nothing serious, no; still, worth knowing about.

He opened the file.

The first problem had to do with the garden. Although it was on sale along with the house, and had the same owners as the house, the patch of land that led from the front door to the gate belonged to someone else. We blinked. How was this possible? The piece of land in question was about the size of a large sofa.

Marco Rossi smiled again. The reason for this peculiar situation, he explained, was that the land around the house had originally belonged to a widow who had died without leaving a will. As she had eighteen legitimate heirs, the land had then been divided into eighteen parcels. Although seventeen of the owners had agreed to sell when the real-estate agent and his wife had bought the garden, one had held out. Not that it mattered: He was very nice, a good friend of Marco Rossi's, in fact, and had promised that he would never object to our crossing over his land in order to reach the garden. Still, if there ever was a "discussion" with the owner, there was an entry to the garden from the other side.

But wouldn't it be simplest, we asked, if he sold us the land?

What's the point of that? Marco Rossi asked. Why spend the money? (For that matter, though, why had the man held on to a piece of land on which he could never build and that was far too small to cultivate?)

He turned another page in his file. Problem two, he said, was the basement *(cantina)*. It, too, did not belong to the owners of the house, but to an old woman who lived down the street, and though she *would* be willing to sell it, she wanted 35 million lire—at that time about twenty thousand dollars.

Anything else?

Oh, yes. If we bought the house, we would have to buy it as two apartments, the upstairs and the downstairs. This was a technicality. Not really a concern, in fact, just something we should be aware of. Indeed, as there were two of us, it could be perceived as an advantage: Each of us could buy one apartment.

More smiles and handshakes. We returned to Rome, where we called Ada. Ada was a real-estate agent. We had met her the summer before in San Francisco, where she was vacationing with her lover Maura, when at a restaurant we had offered to help them translate the menu and then given them tips on where they could go to have a lesbian wedding. Ada immediately summoned us to her apartment, where we showed her photocopies of the documents Marco Rossi had given us to study. It took her about ten minutes to get through them. The reason the house was being sold as two apartments, she said, was because all the major renovations—the staircase, the terrace, the electricity—had been done without permits. The whole house, in other words, was illegal. If we bought it, and the illegal restorations were discovered, we might be compelled either to tear them out (which meant that one apartment would have no bedroom and the other no kitchen or bathroom) or to pay an exorbitant fine in exchange for a *condonno*—quite literally, the issuing of a certificate "condoning" the house's illegality.

"You *could* buy that house," Ada said, "but I wouldn't. I like to sleep at night."

The next day we told our friend Domenico, who would later become our architect, everything that had transpired. "Oh, that sort of thing's pretty common," he said. "In one house I did, I put in an illegal pool. When the town came to check, we just covered the deck with sheets of sod so that the pool looked like a holding tank for water."

Yet another problem with the house was that it cost about twice the going rate for restored houses in Maremma, which was expressed in lire per square meter. Marco Rossi said that this was because the owner had decided to ask for a *prezzo amatoriale*—a "connoisseur's price," the price that someone who loved the house, independently of its actual value, would be willing to fork over.

Again we called Ada. *"Prezzo amatoriale!"* she said. "That's when you buy an apartment on Piazza di Spagna with a view of the Spanish Steps."

The drop of water that made the fountain overflow was a neighbor's enthusiastic description of a ritual that took place every summer in the *borgo* where the house was located: "Most nights everyone eats dinner together at one big table." No fans of bed-and-breakfast communal breakfasts, we knew then that life in that particular *borgo* was unquestionably not for us.

A SHORT time later, Ada called to tell us that she had found the perfect house for us. It was in the center of Assisi and belonged to Maura's sister. We agreed to look at it, rented a car, and drove to Assisi to meet them. The house they led us to turned out to be the most depressing we had seen in all our house-hunting, despite the magnificent vaulted ceiling in the living room. The kitchen was so narrow we could not turn around in it, while the "garden" was about the size of the disputed entrance to the garden in the house near Montemerano.

Uncertain how to proceed, we told Ada and Maura that we would need a little time to think. A few days later, however, an earthquake in Assisi brought down the Giotto frescoes, as well as most of Maura's sister's house. Ada said she dreaded calling us with such dark news, but what could she do? In any case, if we were still interested . . .

"Con bianco non si sbaglia mai"

NOTHING tells you more about a people than their houses. Americans value comfort, the English warmth and coziness, the French eclecticism and good lighting. In Maremma, the ideal is dazzling white walls, shiny granite floors (kept mirror-bright thanks to the chamois-bottomed slippers that the women wear), a ceremonial dining room (but rarely a living room), no lamps but bare bulbs hanging from the ceiling, and a mix of inherited rustic furniture and decidedly "modern" pieces that speak of a remote and faintly unreal urban world.

Italy has gained general prosperity only since the Second World War. A common phenomenon today is to see a wizened old woman in black being driven to the weekly outdoor market in her son's Jeep Cherokee. The once poor try to prove their affluence by living among new things, even if those things are not so fine as the old ones, yet there is more to the story than that: One does not have to look at too many Italian interior design or fashion magazines to see that the country is writhing to free itself from the weight of Renaissance chests and damasks.

Sleek, subdued, and minimal are the order of the day because they deny a suffocating inheritance. This is in no way a criticism, but it goes against what most foreigners want when they come here. Which would *you* rather have, after all: an old farmhouse, or a glossy apartment filled with Perspex and plastic in a brand-new building of poured concrete?

All this is to say that the artisans who worked on our house—Magini the cabinetmaker, Pepe the iron-fitter, Luca and Pierluigi the marble cutters, and Sauro the stonemason—were often incredulous when we told them what we were interested in: a house from once upon a time *(una casa d'epoca)*. (Isn't the whole point of living in Italy, though, to try to live—although one knows that one cannot—in a fairy tale?) We wanted rough terracotta floors, exposed beams, and a *pietra serena* fireplace because the United States does not have anything approaching the same depth of recorded history as Italy: Centuries are to Italy what decades are to us. In short, Americans want old houses because we do not have enough history, whereas Italians want new houses because they have too much of it.

No doubt the biggest question on the mind of the community was this: Which color would we paint our walls? When asked her opinion, Gigliola, who owns the bakery in Semproniano, advised white: "You never go wrong with white," she said. *(Con bianco non si sbaglia mai.)* Sauro put in for white, too. We knew, however, that white was the last thing we wanted, since it makes anything that is not white look dingy. (Perhaps for this very reason, white is the thing here: It gives a woman the chance to show what an immaculate house she keeps.)

In any case, we very much liked the paints made by an English company called Farrow and Ball, which not only had memorable names but came with stories (an appealing idea to writers): Dead Salmon ("The name comes from a painting bill for the Library at Kedleston of 1805") and India Yellow ("produced by reducing the bright yellow urine of cows fed on a special diet of mango leaves"), Sugar Bag Light ("very like the blue of paper used for lining drawers in the late 18th century") and Mouse's Back ("very useful as an early 18th century colour"), Sutcliffe Green ("Connoisseurs often cite green as being the ultimate colour to hang pictures on") and Ointment Pink ("similar to the Regency scheme in the Entrance Hall and Staircase at Castle Coole"). One cannot judge a paint only by its name, however, and in the end we settled on Single Cream, number 9809 in the catalogue. For the trim work we chose the elegantly concise String ("One of a series of pale earth pigment based colours which have been in continuous use either as an off white with brighter colours or as its own colour with a brighter white").

After about three weeks—long weeks, indeed, since we had only to have the walls painted before we could move in—the paint arrived from England, and Sauro began applying it. We were staying at Domenico's vacation house in Todi at the time. One morning Sauro called us. "I'm not sure about this color," he said. "It's a little orange." Although we assumed he was exaggerating because the paint wasn't white—to his eye, we surmised, the ever-so-faint blush that had drawn us to Single Cream might well appear orange—we agreed to drive over and have a look. Upon arriving, we discovered that in our bedroom the ceiling, every wall, and the inside of the closets had been painted the color of a blood orange. What we had taken to be an overstatement proved to be an understatement: *This* was not Single Cream. Instead, according to the label on the cans, this was number 98*16:* Halassah.

After that, frantic calls to London were made, profuse apologies tendered, a promise extracted from the one Italian in the shipping department that the proper paint would be on its way to Tuscany that very afternoon. But in the meantime where were we to live? The day before, Domenico's wife had phoned to inform us rather crisply that we would have to clear out that weekend: They were coming to the country and bringing guests. To make matters worse, the May First holiday was approaching—the most traveled weekend of the Italian year, during which hotel rooms are virtually impossible to come by.

It was a dire time.

We revived, of course. The May First holiday we spent traveling in the deep south, where tourists rarely venture. Sauro reprimed the walls and painted them Single Cream. (The closets, however, we instructed him to leave as they were, as a tribute to the episode.)

Later, the adventure of the paint became the source of considerable mirth for all involved. It turned out that Sauro had called several of our neighbors to have a look at the wrong-colored bedroom before we got there. Apparently they had all shaken their heads in great perplexity and said something to the effect that "these Americans certainly have different taste from ours." They, too, were more than a little relieved when the Single Cream arrived.

Olimpia

BECAUSE we had been living for half a dozen years in furnished or semifurnished apartments when we bought Podere Fiume, we owned almost no furniture. Indeed, all we had was a cornflower-blue sofa; a pair of leather library chairs, both of which we intended to put in the living room; a desk with chestnut legs and a top of Ligurian *pietra serena;* a Bukhara carpet; and four neo-Gustavian chairs with unupholstered seats. In Rome, we had had a Philippe Starck dining table with a heavy green glass top, the corners of which draped downward like the folds of a tablecloth. One afternoon a few months before we moved, however, David, rushing to answer the phone, slipped on the wood floor and crashed into the table, breaking off one of the corners. So that was the end of the glass top. (Later, we moved the base to Podere Fiume and had a local carpenter affix planks of chestnut to it: The resulting table now sits in our garden, and we eat at it in the warm months.)

In short, it was evident that we were going to have to buy some furniture. But where to shop? True, we already knew we didn't want to fill the house with bread chests and dark walnut cupboards of the sort so commonly associated with the word *Tuscan;* at the same time, the crisp functionality of most contemporary Italian furniture—all that brushed chrome and plastic, those sofas with their unbroken expanses of monotonal fabric—left us rather cold. Unlike those Italians who longed to escape the weight of history, we wanted to construct a future for ourselves—or rather, construct a past based on our own private notions of comfort, upon which we could glance with pleasure in some hypothetical future.

This was how we ended up buying furniture from Olimpia Orsini. An interior designer of some repute in Rome, she also owned a little shop that she refused to call a shop—it was her "studio," she insisted—on Via del Boschetto, not far from where we lived. A few months later, she moved her "studio" to a new location, a small street just off Via Margutta, where all the most expensive antique stores in Rome are located, and had business cards printed on which she gave the address as "Via Orto di Napoli (Via Margutta)." Such a street name must have seemed providential to her, for she herself was Neapolitan. Her age was difficult to determine—somewhere between forty-five and sixty, we estimated. She had long dark-blond hair, wore Chanel suits even in the most inclement weather, and smoked incessantly. Her husband, Puccio, was a retired Alitalia pilot—"the sort of man," Domenico said, "who always has four or five million lire in his pocket"—and such was his devotion to Olimpia that rather than relaxing in his retirement, he spent most of his time driving around Rome on a Vespa, doing laborious errands for her. "Puccio," she might instruct, "take these chairs over to Luigi's workshop to be re-covered."

"*Si, bella,*" he would answer, and then, while we watched in awe, bundle a pair of gilt-trimmed Empire armchairs that Olimpia had just picked up in Parma onto the back of his Vespa and zoom off with them. They also had a son in his early twenties, whom we never saw. "I could never have a daughter," Olimpia told us once. "I like being the only hen in the coop."

Olimpia was a terrific snob. A year or so later, we asked Renato, the aristocracy-obsessed owner of the antique shop at the Terme di Saturnia, if he knew her. "The Contessa Orsini?" he asked excitedly, reminding us that the Orsinis were a noble Tuscan family, that an Orsini had built the fantastic and eerie statuary garden at Bomarzo, and that there was an Orsini fortress not far from us, in Pitigliano. And yet to these Orsinis, from what little we knew, Olimpia bore the same relation that Tess does to the d'Urbervilles: that is to say, none at all. Though she lived in a grand apartment featured in *AD* (the Italian version of *Architectural Digest*), and spent her summers in Capri and her winters in Cortina d'Ampezzo, she had grown up, for all we knew, in the darkest backstreets of Spaccanapoli. Who could guess? She was not the sort of woman you could ask about her past. Indeed, all that we did know about her past was that Olimpia was not her real name — it was Marilena — and even this fact Domenico's wife Elizabeth had discovered purely as a consequence of having glimpsed her identity card, one afternoon, when she happened to leave it open on the desk of her shop (sorry, "studio"). Elizabeth was at that time not much in sympathy with Olimpia, who had snubbed her on the street when she was walking with some "important" clients. ("I was carrying groceries at the time," Elizabeth added, by way of what she thought might be the explanation.)

What was indisputable was that Olimpia had wonderful, eclectic taste. Her shop was always full of curious and unlikely pieces: Venetian mercury mirrors edged with seashells, bronze lamps with classical figures in high relief, chairs upon the legs of which sea monsters and mermaids disported themselves, panels of antique wallpaper and toile de Jouy. Olimpia upholstered all the furniture in her shop in the plainest muslin. Nothing was dark and no wood was wood-colored. Chairs that she brought into the shop in dreadful condition, muddy from years of neglect, she would "refresh" simply by stitching some dollar-a-meter cotton onto the worn cushions and slapping the wood with white paint. In her fondness for white, if in no other regard, she echoed Gigliola. (Her failure, however, to replace the old horsehair and hay stuffing in some of these chairs considerably distressed Luigi, the upholsterer, who considered them unhygienic.)

It was all a ruse, all smoke and mirrors, but it worked for Olimpia. Whereas at the other shops on Via Margutta things rarely moved—spindly little side tables and escritoires sat for months, years even, their huge price tags collecting dust—at Olimpia's the occupants changed every week. She had found a niche for herself, a middle ground between the heaviness of tradition and the cool of Cassini and Molteni.

From Olimpia we ended up buying a couple of side tables and a derelict but magnificent carved wood-and-gesso eighteenth-century sofa from Venice, which had managed to escape the attentions of her paintbrush by virtue of its extraordinary color, the most subtle of gray-greens (the color of a Venetian canal). We also bought a pair of white armchairs that went into the winter garden—a room forged from an arcaded space intended for the storage of farm equipment—but their stuffing smelled; worse, Tolo, our fox terrier, displayed from the very beginning a great fondness for them, and as we soon discovered, white is not a very practical color if you have a fox terrier and live in the country. Finally we decided to ask Olimpia if she would buy them back, or short of that, sell them on our behalf to someone else, which she did in four days.

For years it had been the dream of one of Olimpia's colleagues in Rome to have his house featured in *The World of Interiors,* which both he and Olimpia looked at assiduously (neither read English) and which Olimpia referred to simply as "*Interior.*" (By the same token, when asked her profession, she usually answered, "*Sono un interior.*") So devoted was Olimpia's colleague to this magazine that he had saved every issue. When finally the colleague had brought his apartment to what he was certain was a point of aesthetic culmination, he had it photographed and sent the pictures to the editor. She rejected them. In his pique, Olimpia's colleague then threw out his collection, just as Italians in the south have been known to throw out Madonnas and other holy relics that have failed to satisfy the very specific prayers that had been made to them.

Pepe

O F ALL the craftsmen who worked on Podere Fiume, the most entertaining was Pepe the iron-fitter. A short, chubby, balding, yet slightly foppish man (he would often wear an ascot while soldering), he always seemed as rumpled and stale as if he had just come off a transatlantic flight. Pepe was a Roman, and thus a curious blend of the man of the world and the vulgarian. In one sentence he could tell you about the *giardino d'inverno* he had built for Valentino and lament that he had not had "a good shit" *(una bella cagarella)* in ages. We were curious about his wife, and got this assessment from Domenico: "She's pretty elegant, for him."

Pepe had very personal and very definite ideas about food. Vegetables and fruits were bad for you, he believed. Thus his diet consisted entirely of meat, pasta, wine, and coffee (always with cognac). He was also incredibly, even recklessly generous in offering the last of these. Pepe was a fixture at a certain bar on Via Cavour, not far from his studio near Trajan's Forum, and there he insisted on buying a coffee for each and every friend of his who happened to walk in or whom he might have chanced to encounter and co-opt on the way. On average, each of his visits (and he made at least five a day) cost him fifteen thousand lire. To simplify matters, he kept an account at the bar, so that he had to settle up the bill only at the end of the month. But the size of that bill! An average of 75,000 lire a day comes to 2,250,000 lire per month. Multiply that by twelve, and you will find that Pepe's offers of coffee set him back about fifteen thousand dollars per year.

Like all true artisans, Pepe was self-dramatizing. His work, he would say, was not like anyone else's. Although certain things might look simple, such as the wrought-iron brackets for the curtain rods, they required enormous effort and concentration to make. For this reason, he could hardly be expected to work more than two or three hours a day: Only an automaton could work eight or ten hours a day. If lunch was particularly satisfying, perhaps he would be able to put in another half hour's work during the afternoon. In any case, he would need to have a short rest first.

Still, in six months, he managed to complete all our ironwork: grates for the downstairs windows, three sets of doors, arched doors for the winter garden, railings for the stairs (a design copied from a terrace on a crumbling building in the Monti neighborhood of Rome), and finally the curtain brackets and rods. Although Sauro and his assistants, Giampaolo and Fabio, were able to install the window grates and doors, Pepe insisted that he had to come up to install the railings himself.

We had set Pepe up at a country bed-and-breakfast *(agritur-*

ismo) run by Sauro's cousin, but it would not do for him. Instead he decamped to the small hotel in Semproniano, where—and doubtless this was only incidental—all of his meals could be placed on account. (At the *agriturismo,* only breakfast was provided.) During the three days he was there, he worked a total of eight hours. Because Sauro and his crew put in a good ten hours a day five (and sometimes six) days a week, they did not quite know what to make of Pepe and his ascots. They concluded that he was simply "a character" *(un personaggio)* and *said* they enjoyed having him around. He also brought his good cheer to Semproniano, where he not only made friends with the local iron-fitter and other artisans, but invited them all to have dinner at the hotel as his—that is, our—guest. When we went to the hotel a few days later to settle Pepe's bill, we discovered that he had also bought his friends the finest Tuscan wines every night, including a superb 1985 Brunello di Montalcino that we ourselves were thinking of drinking on the eve of the millennium.

WE NOW go to Mauro, the iron-fitter in Semproniano, whenever we need to have anything made, and even Pepe himself would be hard pressed to deny that Mauro is, as T. S. Eliot described Ezra Pound, *"il miglior fabbro."* *

One Saturday morning, about nine-thirty, we took one of Pepe's curtain brackets to Mauro and asked him if he could make five copies of it. He said that he could, of course, but that he

---

*Mauro's wife, meanwhile, operates the gas station next to his shop. In Maremma, old women often "man" the pumps. At one, in Catabbio, the elderly owner stays in her cozy-looking house and only comes out when a car pulls up.

would need a little time. "Certainly," we answered. Rome, after all, was not built in a day. "I can't have them ready until lunch," he said apologetically.

He did have them ready, and all together they cost less than a 1985 Brunello di Montalcino.

Merenda

I F THERE is an image of Sauro and the boys who work with him that sticks in our minds, it is of the three of them having their snack *(merenda)* at about ten-thirty every morning. In the winter, they would sit in the sun on the south side of the house, eating sandwiches of prosciutto on unsalted Tuscan bread, drinking water out of bottles, and, as often as not, not talking. In the summer, Giampaolo and Fabio would take off their shirts and sit in the shade of the pine tree between the house and the *oliveto*—again, not talking. Both of them were very skinny, especially Giampaolo, which is surprising only in that according to our neighbor Delia, who happens to be his grandmother, in his infancy he was a *ciccione*. She has pictures to prove it: an enormous baby, already wearing glasses at eighteen months.

Not long after finishing the house, Fabio went to work near Sovana, where he lives. He was replaced by Gabriele, a boy from Semproniano who was also something of a beanstalk. Like Fabio, Gabriele was inclined to be quiet: A certain reticence, especially on the part of men, is very common here, even seems to be perceived as a sign of dignity. In this regard Gabriele was the epitome of Carducci's Tuscan Maremma, a sweet but exacting land from which the narrator has inherited the habit of harshness— but a gentle harshness.

Magini

AGINI, the cabinetmaker, was a voluble Roman in his mid-seventies: proud of his work, and good at it, though apparently rather bored after half a century's labor. For him, food was much more interesting than wood. He was the archetypal paterfamilias as well as the archetypal gourmand, and really lived for those occasions when all of his family, unto its furthest ramifications, were gathered at his table. Whenever we saw him about the work he was doing for us—to calculate the proper height for the countertops, or to design an armoire or a copy of an eighteenth-century Venetian bookcase that had secret doors on the sides for CDs—it was either just before or just after lunch. One could fairly say that for Magini, work was what he did between breakfast and lunch and lunch and dinner.

Usually we met him at his shop on the outskirts of Rome— which, like every shop of this sort, had a girlie calendar on the wall—and ate with him and Domenico at a canteen in the area. (This is one of the *real* Romes, which would send Miss Lavish from Forster's *A Room with a View* into ecstasies.) The subject of conversation was always food. At one of these lunches we had a particularly good laugh because, just before the waiter came, we were talking about a subject that is considered most inconvenient in Italy: cholesterol. Domenico was saying that according to an article he had just read, fried squid had more cholesterol than practically anything else, even eggs. Just then the waiter stepped up and announced that the "plates of the day" were *spaghetti alla carbonara* and *calamari fritti*. Under the circumstances, no one ordered the calamari, though we all ordered the spaghetti, which was delicious and beautiful beyond words: thin ribbons of pasta the color of a marigold, flecked with almost transparent confetti of pancetta, nested on a pure white plate. "Don't tell Elizabeth," Domenico admonished; "she's on the cabbage-soup diet and I don't want to make her jealous." It seemed that recently one of their daughters had remarked (in charmingly accented English), "Mommy looks as if she is going to have a baby out of her butt."

If you had a look at Magini's arteries, you would probably be worried. You might even be horrified. He himself, however, was anything but worried. In fact, he told us, the previous Sunday he and his wife had made tortellini—by hand—for a small family lunch: seven hundred for ten people. Seventy per person. One thought of Blake's proverb: "Enough—or too much." One also thought that Magini's refusal to worry about lipids and so on might not be so foolish after all. This was only a couple of months after an airplane had blown up over Long Island, killing everyone aboard. How many of those souls had denied themselves eggs or ice cream or fried squid the day before they flew, believing that low cholesterol would grant them a long life?

Il camino

ONE RAINY afternoon Sauro and Giampaolo came by to install the iron curtain brackets Mauro had made. When they arrived, a candle was burning in a pewter candlestick on the mantel. Sauro regarded it with perplexity.

"A candle!" he said. "But there hasn't been a power outage."

"It's for atmosphere," we answered. "It makes a nice light."

With an affirmative "Hmm!" Sauro took his tools upstairs. Atmosphere—the sort embodied by a candle burning on a rainy afternoon—means less to him than it does to us. Thus everything in his own house is brilliantly, one might even say hectoringly, functional—a far cry from the Italian country house of dreams, where worn armchairs and wooden footstools sit gathered around the immense fireplace that is always ablaze and crackling, giving the space a center around which to cohere.

Podere Fiume had no fireplace when we bought it. In the kitchen, which would later become David's study, there was only the little Zappas wood-burning stove, useful for cooking as well as providing heat, if it had worked, which it didn't: This, we soon

32

learned, was what most people used in Maremma. And yet we wanted a *real* fireplace, one that we could sit in front of on cold afternoons, reading or listening to music while Tolo slept on the warm floor. Perhaps because he came from the southern port of Bari and had been educated in California, Domenico understood this longing for the hearth that in English is paired with home. In his house in Todi, he had put fireplaces not only in the living room and dining room, but also the kitchen and two of the bedrooms. "When we're there in the winter, it's so nice and toasty," he said, taking as much pleasure in his command of American idiom as in the toastiness itself. We agreed that a fireplace would have to be a priority in restoring Podere Fiume.

As it happens, there is a considerable market for antique fireplaces and fireplace tools in Italy. In the big cities there are even shops that deal exclusively in old *attrezzi:* wrought-iron pokers; Renaissance andirons; enormous cast-iron plaques decorated with heraldic motifs or mythological figures, to be mounted on the back of the fireplace to throw heat forward; medieval hooks from which to hang the pots in which hundreds of years ago cooks prepared stews of meat and onion and those flecked broad beans called *borlotti.*

Our fireplace came from a man who salvaged them from villas in the mountains between Florence and Bologna. It was made of *pietra serena* and had the year of its making incised on one of its flanks: 1803. It consisted of six pieces of stone: a mantel, a plinth that held up the mantel, and four side pieces to support the plinth. As a base (the poetic hearth), Sauro hauled in enormous stones that had the same color as the fireplace and that a friend of his had chiseled to make fit together. Once constructed, the fireplace measured a meter and a half by a bit more than a meter.

At this point it was midsummer—a hot midsummer at that—and no moment to be building a fire. And so for a few months we filled the fireplace with old patched copper cooking pots, dried wild artichokes; even, for a few weeks, the television set—all the while waiting for the cold weather to come. Indeed, in anticipation of it, we had already bought andirons, a fire screen, and a cord of wood. As a housewarming present, our friend Piero had given us a little stainless steel gadget, a pronged potato roaster designed to be fit into the embers.

At the end of October, the season changed for good; with great excitement we hauled kindling and two armloads of wood into the living room. Armchairs arranged before the hearth, books and lap blankets set out, we went to work. Into the embrace of the andirons went the logs; around their feet kindling and newspaper were stuffed. We lit a match and stood back. Fire! We smiled . . . until the smoke, which at first had spiraled obediently up the chimney, suddenly turned and started filling the room. Tolo slunk away. We threw the windows open. Perhaps there was not enough wind outside to make the chimney draw, we guessed, and we smothered the fire. But the next day, although there was more wind, the same thing happened.

Domenico was called. "Oh, that's normal," he said. "What you have to do is get the chimney warm first. Then it'll draw." Although Mark was dubious, we followed his instructions, stuffing sheets of newspaper up the chimney and lighting them. Again smoke filled the room.

The next day Domenico drove up from Rome with Magini to assess the situation. Along with Sauro, they peered up into the chimney for something like forty-five minutes, hypothesizing in fast Italian. Then they built a fire. A beautiful blaze started, but this time the smoke followed orders and went exactly where it was supposed to. Domenico crowed, just a little. As he turned to leave the room, however, the smoke once again billowed. He scratched his head. Magini scratched his head. Sauro scratched his head. Then we put out the fire and went to lunch.

The problem, Domenico decided over lunch—but why had no one mentioned this possibility *before* the fireplace was built?—was that its opening was too big for the room. (This was exactly the diagnosis Mark had made twenty-four hours earlier.) "A fireplace like that, you need a chimney that's twice as high," Sauro said (but he'd said nothing while building it!), and he proposed to remedy the situation by installing an electric fan at the top of the chimney, the sort that looks like a serrated chef's hat. But no, Domenico interrupted, the solution was to make the opening smaller by attaching a large panel of copper or wood to the back of the mantel. But no, Magini said, the solution was to drape a curtain over the fireplace, far enough away from the fire, of course, so that it wouldn't combust.

Several coffees later we went home feeling rather vexed. So far as we were concerned, none of the proposals on offer was going to do. By chance, while skimming through a design magazine,

David had come across an article about a Danish company called Morsø that made wood-burning stoves. In the illustration accompanying the article, one of these stoves—constructed of black cast iron, with an image of a squirrel embossed on its side—had been placed inside a big fireplace very much like our own.

Well, of course, we thought, that's it, and the next morning we called Domenico. Now, generally speaking, Domenico is the sort of architect who will willingly accommodate the wants of his clients, even when they contradict his own vision. Our house was full of examples of compromise between his aesthetic and ours; indeed, in the whole history of Podere Fiume's renovation, no conflict had ever arisen that had not, in the end, revealed itself to be an opportunity. Yet when we mentioned the wood-burning stove, he reacted with outright horror. "How can you do that?" he cried, as if the mere idea of a stove injured him personally. "I mean, a country house without a fireplace . . . that would be terrible! I couldn't imagine my house in winter without fires going!"

Domenico, for all his gifts, is not a realist. Gently we reminded him that in the case of his own house, he was rarely there in the cold months. We, on the other hand, had a whole winter before us and didn't want to spend it in a haze of wood smoke, our throats sore and the furniture sooty. "Of course not," he agreed, "but that doesn't mean you should do something drastic! We just have to study the problem . . . " ("Study," in Italian, is synonymous with "put off.")

It was obvious that we would have to take matters into our own hands. So we went to Grosseto, where we found a dealer in wood-burning stoves. His shop was full of immense high-tech models, all brilliant enamel and superb efficiency. Mostly he traded in the small stoves that Sauro, Ilvo, and Delia kept in their kitchens, and in the summer he sold pizza ovens. Nonetheless we asked him about Morsø. "The one with the squirrel!" he said, his eyes lighting up like those of the chef at a Chinese restaurant when to his delight a customer asks for duck with taro root instead of chow mein. Of course he knew it! Indeed, the distributor was a friend of his. If we wanted, he could have it for us in three days.

This brings us to now. The stove, which fits perfectly inside the fireplace, is happily burning wood. We hear it crackling. Flames are licking the glass door, and Tolo is asleep on the floor, and Piero's gadget for roasting potatoes—well, it is in a drawer somewhere. Something had to be sacrificed. But Tolo is warm, the house is warm, and if we take off our shoes the stove will warm our feet.

Boredom

THE MOST useful thing anyone living in Italy can learn is how to be bored.

Boredom is part of European life, and even in Paris one has heard it said, "We made love because we were bored, and we were bored making love." But Italy is the most boring of all European countries: Boredom is the nettle among its laurels.

Sundays are boring days in the cities because all the shops are closed (although, *poco a poco,* this is changing). The summer is boring because all the movie theaters are closed (the pleasure of passing a hot afternoon in the dark of an arctic multiplex is unknown here), and for at least a month (August) *everything* is closed. (Truly it is like a month of Sundays.) And just how boring the after-dinner routine can be was brought home to us by an advertisement we saw one summer in Rome: A dramatic alternative to the ritual of dinner, walk, and ice cream *(cena, passeggiata,* and *gelato)* was proposed: *cena, passeggiata,* and *grattacheccha* (grated ice flavored with syrup; essentially a snow cone). Every January or February, Italians take their obligatory "white week" *(settimana bianca)* in the Dolomites or Italian Alps. Christmas is always spent with relatives *(i tuoi)* and Easter with whomever you want *(chi vuoi)*. In Rome you eat gnocchi on Thursday and fish on Friday. In all of Italy you can find delicious fried sweets during the Carnival season, but only during the Carnival season. In short, it is not so much the ritualization as what might be called the "habitualization" of Italian life that makes it so boring.

And yet here you grow to love boredom, even to cultivate it; not to be made restless and frustrated by it. If you are bored to annoyance, it is only because you are taking no initiative, making no use of your own resources. Just as children were much better off when they played with dolls and wooden blocks rather than with Sony PlayStations, such old-fashioned diversions as reading, listening to music, gardening, painting, doing jigsaw puzzles, cooking, and playing with the dog have as much, if not more, to recommend them than the Pandora's box of the virtual world. (The other day, we saw a Land's End catalogue the cover of which was a list of New Year's resolutions: One of them was to read a book through to the end.)

In a boring country, you find that you are content more often than happy, since we make our own contentment and happiness makes itself. In Florence, the name given to that sense of being overwhelmed—even made unwell—by beauty is Stendhal's syndrome. One can suffer from a similar malady here. Beauty is one of its causes, though not the principal one: Its principal cause is the sense of colliding with a happiness in the cosmos that seems endless, and that comes almost as a breeze or a descended magical cloud. This is boredom's antonym.

Il giardino

WHEN WE bought Podere Fiume, it was sur-
rounded by Arizona cypresses, American imports
that proliferate in Italy because they grow fast and provide a
barrier against the winter winds and the scirocco. Unfortunately,
they are also ugly, lacking in the somber discipline of the cypresses that appear as so many black-green flames on the Florentine landscape. This was why we asked Loando to cut them all
down before we moved into Podere Fiume, even though we knew
it would leave the house more exposed and leave us feeling, on
windy nights, like residents of Wuthering Heights. Domenico
supported this decision as heartily as he had opposed the stove;
so did Walter Branchi, the retired musicologist from whom we
had bought our first rosebushes. And so one afternoon Loando
arrived in his harvest-gold Ape, or "bee"—one of those curious
three-wheeled trucks so popular in rural Italy—to cut down the
Arizona cypresses. Two *ragazzi* were coming to help, he said,
and ere long the "boys" arrived—boys who turned out to be, like

Loando himself, in their seventies, but no less hale for the years.
(Considering that he had had his stroke only two months earlier,
Loando was the very picture of health, with bright blue eyes and
a shock of vivid white hair; indeed, so famous was Loando's crin-
atory adornment that during the hunting season his fellow *cac-
ciatori* joked that they often mistook him for a stray sheep.)

Although logic dictated that we finish clearing the yard before
we started planting, we felt that to make it ours we had first to
put out one thing: a rosemary bush that we had bought at the
nursery *(vivaio)* at La Parrina. Then we resumed our work. There
were about three hundred pounds of old barbed-wire fence to be
rolled and hauled away—extremely cautiously. There were rot-
ten fence posts to be dug up and a dovecote in the *porcellaio* to be
torn down. The earth hid innumerable stones, some as large as
watermelons, which we spent hours digging up and collecting in
the hope that they might contribute to the construction of our
fireplace. (Alas, they proved too irregular to be of use to Sauro,
though ideal for Plan B—a rock and cactus garden, in homage to
a rose and cactus garden we had once seen on Capri.)

Finally, the lawn was choked with towering wild fennel, wild
artichokes, and spiny nettles, which, when we pulled them up,
proved to conceal among their roots all manner of artifacts from
Loando's tenure: a very small high-heeled shoe, an old sweater,
part of a child's toy car (this must have belonged to Loando's son,
who now lived in Vienna), bottles, pieces of broken plates, and
innumerable blue and red shotgun shells. Sifting through this
detritus, we felt like archaeologists, unearthing another age in

which a tiny woman in high heels cooked at the Zappas stove, while outside her husband, for pleasure or for dinner, shot into the distance at wild boars, and her son drove a Matchbox car through the furrowed wheat.

FOR A long time we went to bed early, weary in the way that only manual labor makes one. Then one summer morning we stepped outside and discovered, to our surprise, that the yard had more or less been husbanded and was ready to be made into the garden we had long spoken of. David had always wanted an English garden with neat clusters of pinks and fritillaries, clipped yew hedges, a weeping willow; yet as we quickly learned, to create such a garden you must have water—masses of water—the one element that the Maremma will never have enough of.

Instead of fighting nature, we decided to coöperate with her: to make a Mediterranean garden. That first year, we set out five large trees (an ilex, a cherry, a chestnut, an Aleppo pine, and an oak), rosemary and lavender, flowering sage, hydrangea, pomegranate, fifteen varieties of rose (among them "Adam," "Chianti," "Evelyn," "Gloire de Dijon," "Madame Lambard," "Paul Lédé," "Perle d'Or," and "Sombreuil," their names as intoxicating to us as the names of fabrics), a strawberry tree *(corbezzolo)*, *ginestra,* helichrysum, hawthorn, cyclamens, and myrtle. Mark, who grew up in the Deep South, also set out plants from home—camellia ("Moonlight Sonata" and "Pink Perfection"), crape myrtle, and wisteria—for every garden must have a touch of memory, and in Maremma there is more than a touch of the American South.

From a *fornace* that Domenico recommended in Umbria, we

also bought several earthenware planters adorned in the old-fashioned style with mythological figures and costing about fifty dollars each. (Later we saw more or less the same planters advertised in an English gardening magazine for almost a thousand pounds apiece.) Into the two largest of them, which we set on either side of the living-room doors, we put bougainvillea; into the smaller ones, pink geraniums, calendula, marjoram, basil, sage, and sprays of tiny hot peppers ranging in color from firecracker red to ivory to eggplant.

Not everything took. The soil here is like clay when it is wet and like terra-cotta when it is dry. The cherry tree died, as did the camellias. Still, we lost much less than we had anticipated, and as we had read in the same gardening magazine that advertised the thousand-pound planters, if you aren't killing things, you aren't trying hard enough.

Daily Bread

Semproniano, home to about six hundred souls, sits 622 meters above sea level, overlooking the valley of the Fiora River. The oldest and highest part of the village is medieval (until a few decades ago it was called Samprugnano), a clutter of dark stone houses piled on their hill like luggage at a station. Then, down from the piazza, the village flattens; the streets widen. It is here, in modern apartment buildings that could not be more remote from the medieval houses of their ancestors, that most of the Sempronianini live today.

Semproniano has no sights of great historical interest, which is one of the reasons we are so fond of it. Indeed, the *Blue Guide* to Tuscany (2d edition) has only this to say of the village:

> **Semproniano** (trattoria *la Posta,* 6km S at Catabbio) is a small town situated high up (600m) and clustered round the ruins of its *Castle* built by the Aldobrandeschi. In the nearby Romanesque church of *Santa Croce* is a Renaissance holy-water stoup and a very expressive wooden medieval Crucifix.

In the Borgo is the *Pieve dei Santi Vincenzo e Anastasio* with a tall bell-tower. Among its 17C paintings is the Madonna of the Rosary by Francesco Vanni (1609) originally painted for the cathedral of Pitigliano. The oratory of the *Madonna delle Grazie,* on the outskirts of town, has recently been restored [as it happens, by Sauro], and its decorated Baroque interior is typical of the district.

In short, no Caravaggios, no Giottos, no Della Robbia babies. Brunelleschi never worked here; neither did Leonardo.* And yet the town has sat on its hill for a long time, and at certain times of the day it looks as if it might have been painted by De Chirico. (To understand De Chirico well, you have to know Italy on a summer Sunday afternoon, when everything is shut up.)

Semproniano's principle bar is the Bar Sport, and it is here that we begin our day, in the Italian fashion, with a cappuccino. Miranda and her sons, Alberto and Stefano, run the bar, although it has always been her dream, so far unrealized, to expand it into a trattoria. (The boys' father was killed in a hunting accident several years ago.) In contrast to his brother, Alberto is vain and never comes to work looking less than immaculate: Indeed, he is always scrupulously shaved, cheeks glowing, hair perfectly cut, dressed in a blazing white shirt and pressed black pants. (Catia, the veterinarian, recently joked that Alberto wouldn't allow dogs in the bar not because he worried that they would bite him but because he didn't want them to get hair on his cuffs.)

With Alberto we have a lighthearted relationship. For in-

*A Sempronianino designed the *porta santa* at the Vatican, however.

stance, when we come into the bar in the morning, he usually smiles at us and says, *"Mazzafegato?"* (*Mazzafegato* is a local sausage made with the bloodiest cuts of pork.) *"Mazzafegato,"* Mark replies, and is handed a Danish filled with cherry jam. David opts for a Danish with capers, and is handed one with raisins. Sometimes Alberto tells us that, as he has run out of milk, he will have to use goose milk for our cappuccinos. Or he complains about his tropical fish, which have failed to live up to his expectations of them; if they don't start to behave in a more interesting way *(comportare bene)*, he will throw them into the frying pan and eat them.

Although coffee in the country is rarely as good as it is in the city (and coffee in Rome or Florence or Milan is *never* as good as it is in Naples, in no small part thanks to the water), the coffee at the Bar Sport is the best to be had around here. If you are determined to eat a classic Italian breakfast, then you'll have your coffee or cappuccino with a *cornetto*—the Italian version of a French croissant, though much sweeter. Normally bars in rural Italy serve only two or three kinds of *cornetti:* with nothing inside *(vuoti), con marmellata,** and sometimes in the winter, wholegrain ones filled with honey. In the city, of course, bars attached to pastry shops offer more variety—delicate sandwiches of sweet salami and boiled egg, or small pies of almond and chocolate.

---

*Ordinarily the *cornetto con marmellata* is made with apricot jam; no one in any bar has ever been able to give us a good reason why. *"Tradizione,"* people say. (Recently, however, a French friend suggested that apricot was probably used because it was one of the few jams that does not disintegrate in the heat of an oven.)

When we need these flavors, we drive to Castel del Piano, forty minutes away. At the Bar Sport, by contrast, the only innovation of late has been the addition of the *danesi* to the roster, and this is entirely thanks to Semproniano's ambitious young baker, Fabiano, who recently attended a trade show in Rimini.

The Bar Sport at about eight in the morning is the place to be in Semproniano. Rosaria, the doctor, is usually there, having just dropped her daughter off at school; because she is the doctor, she hasn't paid for her own coffee in years. Then there is the man with the moles who looks as if he just stepped out of a painting by Brueghel, and who is known as "the mayor of Le Rocchette," Le Rocchette being a tiny *borgo* three kilometers away. Fabiano himself (Gigliola's son) may be at the bar—just for a coffee, since he starts work at 2:00 A.M.—as well as the man who looks exactly like the guy on the "Get out of jail free" card in a Monopoly set, and the mob of old ladies *(le donnine)* who stop in while doing their shopping and fight over the bill, and finally the few taciturn old Maremmani who are always to be found at the Bar Sport, and who have a glass of hooch with their pastry instead of coffee. On quiet mornings you may encounter three of them sitting on the three bar stools, asleep.

After breakfast comes shopping; the piazza, around which most of the shops are clustered, is also a genial meeting place. (One of the neat things about tiny Italian towns is that their piazzas often bear the same names as hugely famous ones in big cities. Semproniano's is the Piazza del Popolo.) Here we will sometimes run into Sauro's wife, Silvia, peripatetic in her pumpkin-colored Fiat 500, buying bread after taking her son Ettore to school. Perhaps she'll have stopped at the bar to get her lottery ticket in the hope that she, too, will have the luck enjoyed by the anonymous Sempronianina who recently won 202 million lire (about $100,000) in the Superenalotto. Or perhaps she'll be at the kiosk, buying her newspaper from Pietro, whose little shop boasts—in addition to cigarettes, teen-idol magazines, and those maddening *marche di bollo* that Italian bureaucracy requires one to affix to every official document—a single revolving bookcase displaying, alongside the latest works of Danielle Steel and John Grisham, translations of Proust, Schopenhauer, Stendhal, Oscar Wilde, and Virginia Woolf. The kiosk, at about 8:45, when the newspapers have just arrived, is a mob scene. On a recent morning, waiting for our *Herald Tribune,* we ran into Maria Pia, mother-in-law of Rosaria and the Source of All Knowledge in Semproniano. Having recently learned that we were writers, she told us that as a girl she had loved to read but that her mother had warned her that reading would make her go blind. In any case, she said, people in those days were too poor to buy their own magazines: Instead, every month, all the women in the village would pool their resources to buy a single copy of *Grand Hotel,* which would be passed from hand to hand over the course of the month. (*Grand Hotel* is still published and still features the old-fashioned genre known as the *fotoromanzo:* a soap opera in pictures featuring beautiful and distressed "actors" and arranged like a comic book.)

Next to the kiosk is Carlucci, the grocer, whose shop faces Gigliola's bakery. It is here that we go for our *grana padano* (a cousin of parmesan), our mozzarella from Caserta (Silvia's hometown; we once witnessed her stealing the Caserta phone book from the Bar Sport), our Acqua Panna (to be drunk out of the glass Loando left at the house), and when nostalgia for the States gets the better of us, a Kit Kat or a box of M&M's. Most important, there is lots of talk at Carlucci, where three generations work.

Gianni, the handsome son-in-law of Aldo, the owner, comes from Certaldo, near Florence. A few weeks before his wedding to Aldo's daughter, Cristiana, we received an invitation to their *rinfresco*—a term with which we were then unfamiliar but which translates, more or less, as "reception." (Receptions are held after marriages, however, while *rinfreschi* precede them.) In this case, the *rinfresco* took place in the parish hall of the new church, a rectangular, gymnasium-like building with travertine floors and fluorescent lighting that dates from the Ente Maremma. (For the sake of atmosphere, their marriage was going to be solemnized in the old church mentioned in the *Blue Guide.*) Long tables had been set up for the guests to eat at, as well as a buffet that took up the entirety of one wall, featuring sandwiches, salamis, hams, cheeses, cakes, cookies, jam *crostate,* and those peculiar dry biscuits, flavored with anise and olive oil, that are so mysteriously beloved in this part of the world. What struck us most about this *rinfresco* was that it appeared to be less an occasion to congratulate *i promessi sposi* than to "tie on the feedbag." In fact, many of the guests had their *rinfresco* take-out, as napkins and plastic wrap had been provided for this very purpose. Signora Idia, the retired owner of a once-famous *gelateria* in whose garage we were then storing most of our furniture, greeted us upon our arrival, which was apposite, as it was from her that we had first heard the word *rinfresco.* "I'm going to a *rinfresco,*" she had told us, which we took to mean that she was going to the beauty parlor or to some kind of health farm. (This is an example of what Italian teachers call the "false friend.")

Aldo himself is a repository of local history. Thanks to him we know that once upon a time, at Christmas, a kind of *bocce,* with the victor receiving a small purse, was played here—except that instead of *bocce* balls one used a *panforte,* a rock-hard cake from Siena. Thanks to him we also know that once upon a time, when the *tombola* (an Italian version of bingo) was played in Semproniano, dried beans were used to cover the numbers, since *tombola* cards equipped with little plastic windows had not yet been invented. Thanks to him, finally, we know that the old cure for bronchitis is to drink red wine into which a glowing-hot iron has been plunged.

Aldo is famous in Semproniano for what is known in the United States as "suggestive selling." That is to say, he is vigorous in his advocacy of certain new products of doubtful gastronomic merit—particularly as their expiration dates near. Most memorable was a mysterious log of gummy cheese rolled jelly-roll style around sheets of boiled ham and fatigued olives. (Although he insisted that the log was *"favoloso,"* it has never again been seen in his refrigerator case.)

With his thick hair and pencil-thin mustache, Aldo looks like the typical 1950s Italian film star. His father, Sirio, who is in his seventies, is more classically handsome, with cold blue eyes and an impressive nose. Years ago he directed an *orchestrina* in the town. His wife, Elda, was a great beauty then and speaks often of how much she liked to dance. (Today, occasions for dancing—at least the sort of dancing that Elda likes—are all too rare. She is still beautiful, however.)

Often Elda has recipes to dispense. Last summer, when we felt that we had eaten all the tomatoes, all the zucchini, all the pesto that we could stand, she proposed that we make *reginette* (a ribbon-shaped pasta with crenulated edges) with ricotta and *mentuccia,* a kind of wild mint. The recipe is simple: You cook the pasta, then toss it with fresh ricotta (ideally made from goat's milk), chopped *mentuccia* (or another kind of mint), and a tablespoon of the water in which the pasta was cooked. At Christmas the same dish is prepared with the addition of a sprinkling of cinnamon.

Occasionally we also run into Aldo's grandmother, a vigorous woman of ninety-six whom nothing gets past.

WE USED to go to the butcher in Saturnia, but gave up as a consequence of the many elderly ladies and tourists who shopped there. As the ladies in particular had a tendency to buy tiny quantities of a great many meats—a single slice of prosciutto, one sausage, half a chicken breast, two *etti* of ground beef—we often had to wait as long as forty-five minutes to be served. On other occasions, we discovered that where food was concerned, "a little" *(un po')* could mean quite a lot indeed. For instance, one afternoon a large woman from Bologna asked for *"un po' di salsiccina."*

"How many?" Vito, the butcher, asked.

She hesitated. "Eighteen," she said.

Impatience, then, first prompted us to try Andrea, the young butcher who had set up in Semproniano. His shop provided an altogether more pleasant (not to mention speedier) experience. All the meat that Andrea sells is raised at a small *azienda* a few kilometers from Semproniano. (In Tuscany, the feeding practices that led to Mad Cow disease were never taken up.) Among his specialties is an extraordinarily good pancetta from just over the hill in Cortevecchia, and *capicollo,* a fennel-seasoned salami made from the neck of the pig. That Maremman taste is not necessarily our taste, however, was brought home to us the morning we saw displayed in Andrea's gleaming glass case the brains, lungs, heart, and liver of a lamb, to be eaten fried. (This is a favorite dish of Maria Pia's.)

MARKETING in Rome was a lot less pleasant, in part due to the Romans' anticlerical sentiment: No one anywhere appreciates those who take advantage of their station, particularly when these advantage-takers are clergy and ostensibly above worldly things. Once, in a popular *salumeria* on Via Merulana, an old nun flouted the etiquette that requires customers to take a number by demanding the immediate attention of the shopkeeper. When he asked her number and the good sister replied that she didn't think it was necessary for *her* to have one, the man laughed, as did all the other customers. "You'll have to wait, just like everyone else, *suora,*" he said. "But your patience will be rewarded in heaven."

Old nuns are feeble or ferocious, as need be: feeble when they want to be given a seat on a crowded bus, ferocious when food shopping. Priests seem to maintain better relations with the secular world, although a daring film titled *Pianese Nunzio* portrayed a priest in Naples who stood up to the Mafia even as he sodomized the thirteen-year-old hero. (Perhaps a more apposite title for the film would have been *Sodom and Camorra.*) We never saw a priest try to butt ahead in a *salumeria.*

FROM Semproniano, we go to Saturnia to collect our mail. On the Fibbianello, the road that links the two towns, is a small refuge for injured or abandoned animals run by the World Wildlife Fund. The occupants here include peregrine falcons, hawks, several varieties of owl, a tamed fallow deer *(daino)* that rubs its velvety antlers against your leg, two wolves that are fed entire lamb carcasses and whose area of the refuge is littered with wool and bones, and lastly a baby wild boar to which Elda feeds milk each day from a bottle. There is also, curiously enough, a pair of obese raccoons that stowed away on a ship from Canada, escaped for a while into the port city of Livorno, and were eventually brought here. Raccoons do not exist in Italy—yet. Recently we brought some Canadian friends to see the refuge, and Brunella, who volunteers there, asked them if they might be willing to bring the raccoons home with them: *alla loro patria.*

When we first started living here, we tried having the mail delivered to a box at the end of the road, but this did not work out very well. Owing to the intricacies of the Italian postal service, mail for Podere Fiume had to be routed through Santa Caterina, quite a distance away on an extremely curvy road. In those days, the road between Santa Caterina and Podere Fiume was still unpaved, so if it was raining or cold, or if the postman thought there was not enough mail to justify the effort, he would sometimes not bother to come at all. Once he even taped a note to our box informing us that on his last visit he had seen a wasp crawl into the opening and would therefore not deliver any more mail until we promised to meet him at the mailbox and prove that there was no longer a wasp's nest inside. And yet, so inconsistent is the Italian postal system that sometimes the mail *was* delivered during a storm and so arrived sopping wet.

The last straw—which in all fairness had nothing at all to do with the post office in Santa Caterina—was this: We found, three separate times in one week, tarantulas in the box.

After that, we talked to Maurizio, the postmaster in Saturnia, and he proposed we take a box *(casella)* there. That way we would not have to worry about wet mail or tarantulas. Also, we would get our mail at least two days sooner, since it would no longer have to be routed through Santa Caterina. Finally, when we were away, our mail could collect safely (and drily) in its box.

The first Christmas we had a *casella,* we gave both Maurizio and Florio, the Saturnia postman, a bag of coffee beans from Tazza d'oro, a famous coffee store near the Pantheon in Rome. After all, in the United States, giving a present to the mailman is simply one of those things you do. Maurizio and Florio, however, were perplexed: Though Italians are not ungenerous people, they are unused to receiving presents and therefore often at a loss as to how to respond to them. The next day when we arrived at the post office to pick up our mail, Maurizio loaded our arms with bottles of olive oil, wine, and grappa from his family's farm—everyone in this part of the world farms at least a little.

RECENTLY Maurizio traded in his battered red Fiat Panda (Fiat Pandas are invariably red or white) for a sleek new silver Audi station wagon. If you wonder at the fact that he is able to afford a seventy-thousand-dollar car on a postmaster's salary, consider this: All his life (Maurizio is in his mid-forties) he has lived with his parents in the *podere* where he was born. He pays no rent, nor does he pay for food. He invests in the stock market. Behind the big house that his parents and uncles have divided into apartments there stands a second house, about five years old, that his parents refer to as "Maurizio's house." It has never been occupied; instead it awaits some hypothetical future when he will have married and had children of his own. (At the same time, he doesn't seem to be looking; instead, he spends most of his afternoons with his friends at the bar in Montemerano. Although Maurizio says he would be happy to marry and have children, our sense is that he would not be unhappy not to.)

Maurizio is typical of a phenomenon that has the Pope worried. More and more adult children in Italy (sons, mostly) are not leaving home. And why should they, when home is so comfortable? The phenomenon is much on the Italian mind. An advertisement for a Roman real-estate agency shows a bearded man diapered in a crib, a pacifier in his mouth, and above his head the legend "Still living with Mommy?" *(Stai ancora con la Mamma?)* The mayor of one southern town has imposed a fine on men over forty who aren't married. The province of Val d'Aosta gives cash bonuses to couples that have babies.

If health is any measure of happiness, then the life that Maurizio's parents lead with him has much to recommend it. Although in his late seventies, his father still works the fields every morning and every afternoon; his mother, in addition to cultivating a flower garden and a vegetable garden, knows the secrets of the forest; she heads out, on March mornings, basket in hand, to hunt those elusive, thin, delicate stalks of wild asparagus that proliferate here in the early spring. One afternoon she showed us vases of the stuff, set out like flowers, waiting to be pickled or eaten with *spaghetti alla carbonara*. She reads, too. Around Christmas one year, we asked Maurizio if the Italians had a word for people who don't like the holiday. We told him about Scrooge in *A Christmas Carol;* he asked if we had a copy of the book to loan him, so that he could give it to his mother. We presented them with an Italian translation, which she read immediately. No, she reported through Maurizio, there was no Italian word for a scrooge.

Although Maurizio has traveled all over Asia and lived in England he knows less about Italy than we do. In this way he is typical of his generation in Italy. Many of the farmers we know, for example, have been to the Seychelles and Mauritius, but never to Milan, and only once or twice to Rome. They are more familiar with Egypt than they are with Puglia; have cruised down the Nile but never visited Lecce, that marvelous city known as the Florence of the Baroque. Their parents, by contrast, have hardly ventured in their lives farther than Grosetto. Once we ran into Maurizio's mother when he was on vacation. "He's in Cuba," she said matter-of-factly, as if Cuba were just on the other side of the hills. In a sense, in Maremma, it is.

Sheep Jams

SOMETIMES in the morning, on the way to Semproniano, we'll encounter a sheep jam. They have a way of appearing when you least expect them, and in the most inconvenient of places—on the other side of a harrowing hairpin turn, say, or on a bridge. We screech to a stop. Tolo, agitated by the rich odor of manure and urine, the music of bleats and baahs, starts to bark madly, then tries to dig his way through the back window. Meanwhile we idle. What else can you do when faced with a flock of forty ewes and a ram or two, their backs draped with coils of yellowing wool like dreadlocks? Sometimes the sheep are alone; more often someone is leading them—an elderly farmer driving an elderly Ape or an old woman on a Vespa. With a smile the shepherd or shepherdess signals us forward—not to drive around but *into* the herd.

The first time we did this it seemed weird, even scary. With every inch we moved forward, we anticipated the moment when the car would touch the sheep: Legs of lamb would flatten under the wheels, wool would fly. And yet, at the crucial instant, the flock did part, as the Red Sea parted for Moses.

This is what passes for traffic here, in this valley where not a stoplight is to be found for miles and miles in any direction.

"The Documents Must Agree"

I N March 2000, the following item appeared in the *Italy Daily*, a supplement to *The International Herald Tribune.* It says much about the poetry and madness of Italian bureaucracy:

> Highway police arrested 10 people late Wednesday in Pescara, charging them with running a fraudulent drivers' school that sold drivers' licenses for up to five million lire each. Another 32 people were accused of participating in what authorities described as a cooperative that drew clients from around Italy, some of whom were reportedly almost blind. Italians frequently complain that obtaining a drivers' license in Italy is difficult without attending costly schools. Foreign residents in Italy for more than one year are also expected to attend the schools and obtain a national license, regardless of their driving record.

For us, the long process of getting licenses began shortly after we bought Podere Fiume. To live in the countryside one has to have a car, and to own a car in Italy one has to have an Italian driver's license. This is simply the law. If you don't have an Italian driver's license, your only options are to ask an Italian friend to buy a car for you, then sign a document giving you the right to drive it, or to bring in a car from another country—yet if you do this, after four months you will still be obliged to replace the foreign license plates with Italian ones, which requires an Italian license.

Many countries have reciprocity agreements for licenses with Italy; the United States, unfortunately, is not one of them, since there is no federal driver's license and it would be bureaucratically untenable for Italy to make separate agreements with each of the fifty states. As a result, even drivers who, like us, have had licenses for almost a quarter of a century are compelled to take the driving test here. In Italian.

Wanting advice, we called Elizabeth, since we knew she had gotten an Italian license several years earlier. "Oh, it was easy," she said. "I just paid someone to take the test for me."

"But how can someone take it for you?"

"Only the oral part. What you do is you pretend you don't speak Italian and explain that you've brought along a translator. Of course he isn't really a translator. You mumble to him, and he answers all the questions. It costs about two million lire."

Neither of us was particularly keen to pay two million lire to a "translator." Nor did we believe that we needed one, even if Elizabeth had. After all, we both spoke Italian. We were good drivers. Also, Mark had managed to survive orals in graduate school: Could a driving test be so much worse than that?

A lawyer we knew now explained to us how to proceed. In order to circumvent the notorious driving schools, we would need to get in touch with an *agente*. In Italy, an *agente* is basically someone who makes his living mediating between bureaucracies and human beings. Little of a practical nature can be done without an *agente,* since the system is so baroque that learning to negotiate even a small region of it requires years of study.

The *agente* the lawyer recommended was named Bruno. He drove a motocycle and wore a cashmere coat. To obtain licenses, he said, we would first have to complete a form *(pratica).* This would cost 200,000 lire. After that we would have to take an eye exam from a doctor who would also affirm that we were in good health. This would cost 150,000 lire. After that Bruno would make an appointment for us to take the *oral* exam. If we passed it, he would make an appointment for us to take the driving test—the one behind the wheel.

Now the comedy begins. First we go to take the eye exam. To our amazement, the doctor who administers it turns out to be, to all intents and purposes, blind. (Perhaps he got *his* license in Pescara.) So far as we can tell, he is able to give the exam only because he has memorized the chart. Indeed, he can barely read our passports through his thick glasses and the clouds of smoke from his cigar.

Once we receive the necessary certificates, Bruno makes an appointment for us to take the oral exam—the *teoria*. When? we ask. In just two months, he tells us. Two months! He smiles, and explains that in France the wait is usually four months. Then he gives us some small pink slips of paper *(foglie rosse)* permitting us to drive during the interval. He also gives us a manual of road regulations to study, along with a book of sample written tests. These tests have a reputation for being almost sadistically difficult, mostly because they exalt the principle of the trick question. An example:

When encountering this sign,

1. One must decrease speed.   TRUE   FALSE
2. One must drive with prudence.   TRUE   FALSE
3. It is forbidden to pass.   TRUE   FALSE

One and two are true. Three, however, is false. When driving through a dip in the road *(cunetta)* it is, in fact, legal to pass, although obviously unwise to do so.

Fortunately, we are not going to have to take the written test—a fact that does not in any way mitigate our anxiety over the oral test that we will have to take. So we study. Both of us, by nature, are studiers, and indeed the exercise proves to be well worth it. After years of driving in Italy, we finally learn the meaning of certain road signs we had previously found to be enigmas:

Obviously it is important to know what signs mean, just as it is important to know the basics of giving first aid to an injured driver or passenger after an accident. On the other hand, the many pages of the manual devoted to right of way *(precedenza)* demonstrated amply why this part of the exam is known as "theory." After all, a drawing such as this one,

illustrating an intersection of five streets in which there is neither a stop sign nor a stoplight nor a yield sign, and requiring the testee to adduce the sequence in which the various cars should give way to one another, has little to do with reality. Intersections of this sort quite simply do not exist, and even if they did, the truth is that in Italy "right of way" belongs to the speediest, the most aggressive, the driver "with balls" *(con palle)*.

Even so, we are determined to master the theory of *precedenza,* not only because we have to but because, as theory, it has its own mysterious allure. We memorize the rules of passing (the most ignored of all on Italian roads), the basic mechanical principles of the car engine, the guidelines on where it is and isn't permissible to park. We learn what the *croce di Sant'Andrea* means and what distinguishes railroad crossings *con barriere* from those without.

The morning of the test, we drive out very early to the *Motorizzazione*—the Motor Vehicles Authority—the offices of which are located far from the center of Rome, on the Via Salaria.* Like

---

*So called because in antiquity it was the route by which salt was brought into Rome.

many municipal buildings in Italy, the *Motorizzazione* is an imposing, ugly structure, its very architecture intended to bully and subdue. The walls are of dirty stone; there are NO DOGS signs posted everywhere. Inside, the light is greasy. The testing room itself, when we peer into it, proves to be a large and windowless trapezoid cluttered with chair-desks of the sort more commonly found in high schools. In a sort of antechamber, a United Nations of examinees sits waiting. Most of them are accompanied by instructors from their driving schools, who quiz them on *precendenza* even as they wait.

David is summoned first to the exam room, along with another American, a language teacher from Chicago who has already failed the test once. They speak in English while the examiner, a prematurely elderly young man rather resembling a stoat, reads through the language teacher's *pratica*. In his case, all appears to be in order. Then the examiner opens David's file, placing his medical certificate alongside his passport. For several minutes he looks from the certificate to the passport, the passport to the certificate. Then he pushes them back across the desk.

"The medical certificate says that you were born in 1971," he says. "The passport says that you were born in 1961."

David laughs. "Oh, that's a mistake. I'm not surprised—you see, the doctor who gave me the eye exam was blind."

No laughter. Not even a smile.

"Also, your passport says that you were born in Pennsylvania USA."

"True."

"But your medical certificate says that you were born in Pittsburgh USA."

"Also true. Pittsburgh is the city. Pennsylvania is the state."

"But they don't agree. They must agree."

Here the language teacher enters the fray, assuring the examiner that David is not lying: Pittsburgh really is a city in Pennsylvania. He goes on to explain, with the remarkable calm of a teacher, that in the United States the state of birth is always given on passports, just as in Italy the city of birth is given. No doubt the doctor put down the city in order to remain in accordance with Italian rules.

"But they don't agree," the examiner repeats. "The documents must agree."

"Pittsburgh is the second-largest city in Pennsylvania," David throws in hopefully.

It is no use. The examiner is intractable. David is ordered out and told to make a new appointment.

When he tells Mark what has happened, Mark looks at his own documents and discovers the same discrepancy: His medical certificate says that he was born in Biloxi, while his passport says that he was born in Mississippi.

In a white rage, we hunt down Bruno. He is as unflappable as the examiner was intractable. First he looks at the medical forms. Then he looks at the passports. "Well, he was right," he says after a moment. "This is the doctor's fault. The documents must agree."

We think about it. We grow calmer. Of course the documents must agree, we acknowledge. There is no reason to be angry with the examiner. He had *ragione.* He was just doing his job.

Only hours later, once we are back at Podere Fiume, do we realize what really happened that morning: For a few moments we had been thinking like Italians.

SIX WEEKS later, we return to the *Motorizzazione* and this time actually take the test. Mark goes first, along with an Arab and an Albanian. For forty-five minutes David watches through an open door while the candidates sit hunched across the desk from the examiner, who makes diagrams in the air with his hands. Not a word can be heard, though if one watches carefully one can see, intermittently, that Mark is laughing.

"Did you pass?" David asks when the three men emerge.

"I am promoted," he says. *(Sono promosso.)*

It is now David's turn. While he and two other candidates—both Romanian—respond to questions in the trapezoid-shaped room, Mark takes on the role of the ancient mariner for those who have yet to be tested. As is common in such situations, tension fosters an atmosphere of intimacy. For a time Mark and the Tunisian woman who works at the Saudi Arabian embassy and the elegant lady from Bangladesh form a little community. Worriedly they listen while he tells them what has been asked (Why is it dangerous to drive quickly on a curve?) as well as what has not (nothing about *precedenza;* a sigh of collective relief is heard).

A quarter of an hour passes. All at once one of the Romanians comes flying out of the room as if he has quite literally been ejected. "He fucked up," a driving teacher murmurs darkly. *(Ha bocciato.)*

"It's the second time, too," says another.

A quarter of an hour after that, his countryman storms out. He, too, has fucked up. David is now alone with the examiner. Another quarter of an hour passes—by now the women are beside themselves with panic—when at last he comes out.

"Anch'io sono promosso," he says. Which means only that he, too, has won the right to take another test.

A few days later, we were talking with Pina and Giampaolo, who run our favorite restaurant in Maremma—Il Mulino in Scmproniano—about the driving test. "Why do they make it so hard to pass?" we asked.

"It goes back to Fascism," Giampaolo said. "The *fascisti* wanted to make the ordinary citizen fearful and dependent on the state."

"And to encourage corruption," Pina added. "Bribery. This way, people who worked for the state could get rich."

The Fascist attitude also led to the invention of a whole industry: the industry of the *agente*.

How odd that we were having this conversation in Tuscany, on a hilltop not far from the sea, on that lovely peninsula that was for centuries quite literally the mother of invention! After all, Italy gave us Leonardo da Vinci and Galileo and Marconi. Now most of that energy has been eaten up by the exigencies of contending with bureaucracy—contending with it, or evading it. If there are no longer poets in Italy, it is because bureaucracy has slayed or absorbed them.

ANOTHER month later and the comedy was finished. (So sings the clown.)

To take the "practical" driving exam, we first had to meet someone called Signor Antonio in the Olympic Village in Rome. Since we had to be there at 8:00, we left home at 5:00 A.M. (How pointless it all seemed, driving to Rome in the dark to take a driving exam!)

Although we had never been there before, getting to the proper piazza in the *Villaggio Olimpico* proved to be a piece of cake. Since we arrived at 7:30, there was time for us to have a coffee before meeting up with Signor Antonio. Light was beginning to creep into the sky, which had an orange cast, later than it seemed it should have. This was the scirocco, the African wind that carries with it the sand of the Sahara; it would worsen as the morning progressed, so that by the time we took the exam it would be necessary to use headlights.

Having had our coffee, and not finding Signor Antonio, we walked around. The architecture of the Olympic Village answered every idea one had of hell. It was in the summer of 1960 that the XVII Olympic Games were held in Rome, and in addition to the dormitories for the athletes, which are now depressing apartments for the down-at-heel (according to a placard, one building had recently been "deratted and disinfested"), other reminders of the event include an unmown park strewn with hypodermics; a granite obelisk bearing the five interlocking rings; streets named for the participating nations, many of which (Yugoslavia, the Soviet Union) no longer exist. There was also a grimly lit pharmacy with a gigantic sign in its front window announcing a special on "Incontinence Diapers." (The Italians do not use euphemisms for this sort of thing. In the United States, by contrast, advertisers prefer phrases like "Adult Hygiene System.")

Presently Signor Antonio arrived in a white Fiat 600. We exchanged pleasantries, after which Mark drove, then David. After half an hour, we were through—or so we thought—for we had been given to understand that Signor Antonio was the examiner. But he was not. As he explained, he worked for one of the more than five hundred driving schools in Rome; his function was not to conduct the exam but to give us a quick "lesson"—which we thought was the exam—and to provide the car for the real exam. In Italy one cannot legally take the exam in one's own car; instead one has to take it in a car specially outfitted with two sets of brakes—one for the driver and one for the forward passenger.

And now the examiner himself arrives. He is a short, misshapen, corrupt-looking man with hair like steel wool. In his arms he carries a thick briefcase that, we soon learn from Signor Antonio, contains the licenses for all the examinees who have been waiting for him. Before beginning his work, though, he must first be taken to the bar for coffee by Signor Antonio and all the other instructors from the driving schools. While they are in the bar, an order for the exams is worked out. There are twelve examinees. We are to go seventh and eighth.

The long and the short of the exam is that one of us passed, the other failed. The one who failed (Mark) was the first one of us to go, and the first American of the day as well. (All of the Asians had already failed.) Halfway into the exam, the misshapen examiner began delivering himself of anti-American invective to Signor Antonio, who was in the car to man the second set of brakes. "Americans think they can come into Italy and get whatever they want," he said. Mark did his best to maintain his cool. "They have to be taught," the examiner continued ominously. Mark indicated two cars that had just run a stop sign, and was ignored. "This American," the examiner said, then broke off to call Signor Antonio's attention to a poster for a female candidate in the upcoming election called Monica Ciccolini and made a rude remark about her person, as well as about the similarity of her name to that of the Italian porn actress Cicciolina. Signor Antonio, meanwhile, had joined cause with the examiner and put in his oar about Americans—even though we had each paid him 100,000 lire to advocate for us.

Why one of us passed and the other failed was a caprice (Mark is a much better driver than David), for the system is designed so that the examiner does not have to be accountable for his decisions. If a passing surge of antipathy toward Americans was his reason for failing Mark, the examiner will face no reprisals. We recalled once again what Pina and Giampaolo had said about the Fascists; for all its rhetoric about "us" *(noi)*, Fascism was deeply divisive. The populace was to be made anxious and insecure, even tyrannized, with the state transformed into an almost Homeric god. In the person of the driving examiner, we met that same sadism: a false and repellent pride in being Italian—and in *not* being Japanese, or Indian, or African, or Canadian—the implications of which were given weight by the recent movement of some citizens in the rich northern part of the country to secede and form a new nation called Padania, by the rise of neo-Fascism in the raiments of Forza Italia, and by the constant pressure of the Catholic Church to sustain a culture of conformism. Nor was the irony of this scene being enacted in the Olympic Village, a forty-year-old monument to an ideal of fraternity, lost on us. For though the Italians are vocal in criticizing their government, the fact remains that Italians have more or less the system they have chosen, and perhaps even want.

There is no charm in any of this. The cloud has no silver lining. One is not made a better person for having had the experience. But cynicism is not the answer; nor, for that matter, is the romanticizing of bureaucracy—a thing to look at unflinchingly, and to be made angry by, and finally to grieve for.

Postscript: One month later Mark took the *pratica* again; he passed.

Caca d'oie

IN THE months just after we bought Podere Fiume and before
the restoration work had begun, we got into the habit of buying and reading design magazines. Our favorites were *House and
Garden* (the English version), *Homes and Gardens,* and *The World
of Interiors.* Sometimes, however, such was our avidity to look at
pictures of houses that after we had finished these we would also
buy *Architectural Digest* and *AD; Elle Decor* (the French, Italian,
and American editions); *Côte Sud, Côte Ouest,* and *Maison Madame Figaro; House Beautiful;* and *Country Homes and Interiors.*
Once we had exhausted these, we would occasionally even turn
to magazines in languages we could not read—Dutch or German—or periodicals treating of subjects we regarded with skepticism, such as *Feng Shui for Modern Living.* Finally, if after all
this we still hungered for pictures and ideas, we would resort to
such doubtful Italian publications as *Brava Casa, Casa Bella,* and
Cose di Casa, the latter in essence a catalogue of brightly colored
kitchen appliances.

Some houses dictate their own decoration. If you buy a Georgian row house in London or an art deco house in Los Angeles or an antebellum mansion in Natchez, chances are that you will end up choosing furniture to match the architecture. Podere Fiume, by contrast, gave us almost nothing in the way of historical direction. When we bought it, after all, the ground floor consisted of animal stalls with concrete floors, while the upstairs rooms had no detailing to speak of; they were simply spaces with windows. Because this was Tuscany, we knew that we wanted to lay terracotta floors, use Carrara marble for the kitchen countertops and wrought iron for the stair rail. Beyond that, though, who knew? There was an overabundance of possibilities. The design magazines displayed all manner of lamps and sofas and wallpapers, many of them ugly or prohibitively expensive, but others, at the very least, suggesting routes we might follow toward the achievement of that ideal, a beautiful and comfortable home.

One of the great pleasures of restoring a house in Italy is that one can take advantage of the tradition of craftsmanship that persists here. In the Monti neighborhood of Rome, the narrow streets are full of upholstery workshops *(tappezzerie)* as well as the *laboratori* of iron-fitters, lamp makers, lampshade makers, woodcarvers, and furniture restorers. When we lived in the United States it would never have occurred to us actually to design and commission a sofa, say, for the simple reason that in the States artisans of the sort who abound in Rome are difficult if not impossible to find (and often Italian); they work exclusively for architects and interior designers; they charge enormous fees. In Italy, on the contrary, it is possible to carry ten meters of fabric into a shop, draw a picture, agree upon a price, and return two months later to find a sofa waiting for you, built down to the piping to your specifications, and costing half of what a new one would at Macy's.

Domenico and Elizabeth first introduced us to Luigi and Francesco Amedeo, the cousins in whose small upholstery workshop on Via del Boschetto all of our curtains and several pieces of our furniture were eventually made. In his early thirties, Francesco was tall and soulful and always wore a long white laboratory coat rather like a doctor's. (Italians love uniforms.) His smaller and more athletic cousin, by contrast, favored muscle T-shirts and tight jeans. Their shop presented a curious mixture of the butch and the effeminate. As at Magini's, a girlie calendar hung over the telephone; at lunch the assortment of half-finished sofas, chairs, throw pillows, and padded headboards was pushed aside to make way for the table at which Francesco and his friends from other shops on the street played poker. (Luigi usually stood aloof from these games.*) At the same time, nothing delighted the cousins more than an opportunity to select *passamanerie,* those trims and ruffles and bobble fringes with which their sofas and armchairs were always so extravagantly festooned. They exulted over blood-red velvet damasks, sofas with ball-and-claw feet, explosive floral silks for ottomans (which the Italians call *poufs*). Their tools of the trade were the saw and the staple gun, but there was also a delicate little sewing machine in one corner at

---

*For a long time we thought that Luigi was gay. Shortly before Christmas, however, when we happened to pass by the shop, Francesco told us that he was on his honeymoon. Apparently it had been a shotgun wedding, as the bride was already several months *in dolce attesa* (literally, "in sweet waiting").

which Francesco could be seen running a seam through a curtain-sized swath of "Roses and Pansies" chintz.

The discovery of Luigi and Francesco led us to the world of furnishing fabrics. One afternoon, while browsing through an issue of *Elle Decor,* David had admired a sofa that was covered in Colefax & Fowler's "Old Rose" chintz. So he called the Colefax & Fowler shop in London to ask for a sample. American experience had led him to expect that upon making such a request, he would be immediately asked if he was a professional or an account holder, then "shown the door." Instead the young woman who answered—the redoubtable Charlotte May-Smith—could not have been more friendly. "Old Rose, oh yes, it's lovely," she said, "I have it in my bedroom," and immediately put a large sample in the mail.

Presently Charlotte became a sort of touchstone for us. As we soon learned, she knew her stuff. She was intimately familiar not merely with the hundreds of fabrics Colefax & Fowler itself produced (Sybil Colefax, one of its founders, was a famed Bloomsbury hostess and friend to Virginia Woolf) but also, it seemed, with the stock of every fabric house in the world: Pierre Frey, Lelièvre, Bennison, Percheron, Claremont, and Rubelli, to name but a few.

From magazines we learned the evocative language of fabrics, a nomenclature easily as seductive as any texture or print: brocade and brocatelle, chenille and horsehair, *lampas* and toile de Jouy and toile de Nantes. Individual fabric names could be equally suggestive. Most of the glazed chintzes, with their sprays of rose and peony, hydrangea and gladiola, had names that evoked the life of English country houses: "Bowood" and "Amberley," "Sissinghurst" and "Sutherland." Linens were called "Lamorna" or "Serge Antique" and came not in white and gray but toast and oyster. Through Charlotte, we obtained samples of "Leopoldine," "Belgarbo," "Couvert de Feuilles," "Ballon de Gonesse,"* "Argentelle," and (perhaps our favorite name) "Solace" in celery. (*Solace in Celery.* It was a poem!) Yet "Solace" also came in parchment, black pearl, crème brûlée, persimmon, and blue sage. In the world of fabrics, reds were tomato or claret, greens were khaki or *caca d'oie* (quite literally, "goose shit," and resembling tarnished copper), oranges were brick, terra-cotta, or cinnamon.

Photographs of fabrics were frequently deceptive. A needlework leopard-spotted weave of which Charlotte, on our behalf, had ordered a sample, turned out to be, in her words, "Cheap and nasty. I chucked it in the bin." By the same token, fabrics that in photographs appeared muddy and characterless could reveal themselves, on closer inspection, to be textural marvels, nubbly to the touch, or mysteriously sleek, or rough like a carpenter's hands. Some, such as the highly pictorial toiles de Jouy, revealed their fascination only when applied in vast quantities, while others were of a delicacy that only the most limited use— as a small cushion, or to cover a single chair—would show to advantage. Prices varied drastically as well, and rarely corresponded to our expectations. Thus richly colorful chintzes, such as the "Old Rose" with which our journey had begun, turned out to be surprisingly affordable. On the other hand, a tapestry

*The Concorde crashed in Gonesse, where once hot-air balloons were launched into the sky.

fabric called "Marly," from the complex greenery of which small red berries occasionally burst, could set you back two hundred dollars for just half a meter. ("Marly" was a bargain, however, compared to a Prelle velvet brocade originally woven for Marie Antoinette's bedroom at Versailles and so expensive that the company has not had a commission for it since the 1950s. They have, however, produced a poor-man's version of this brocade, a warp-printed silk that retails for about $750 a meter. Another Prelle velvet, "La Plume," with a three-tier pile, goes for about $1,600 a meter.)

It was now time to make decisions. After all, a drawerful of fabric samples (and Charlotte had sent us dozens) does not furnish a house. Nor do fabrics that one loves necessarily suit a house's temperament, for houses, even if they lack historical reference, have a way of asserting their own distinct likes and dislikes, and ours, as it gradually came into being, as the stalls became a living room, and the fireplace went up where once there had been only troughs and narrow windows, and a staircase ascended toward the hole Sauro had ripped months earlier out of the downstairs ceiling, now made it quite clear that it had no intention of being draped with chintz.

Eventually we decided (or perhaps we should say the house decided) on a large fawn-and-cream check for the living-room curtains, a cream-and-blue Chinese toile for the bedroom curtain and bedspread, and for the glass doors that opened onto the garden, a linen from Spoleto with a pattern of bees woven into it. From Luigi we commissioned a *capitonné* pouf, buttoned like a chesterfield, to be covered with the first fabric we had ever actually bought: "Briarwood," an Arts and Crafts cotton patterned with flowers, strawberries, and tiny birds. Next came a sofa for one of the studies, amply cushioned and upholstered in a rough Indian cotton (cumin, the color was called) with piping in the same cotton, though this time in turmeric. (This sofa was so large that it would not fit up the stairs; instead, like a piano, it had to be hoisted through the terrace doors with a crane.) For the Venetian sofa we had purchased from Olimpia we chose a mysterious fabric called "Malabar" that managed at once to suggest leopard spots and stripes.

The most troublesome decision, however, concerned curtains for David's study (the one with the enormous sofa). Perhaps because this was the room in which curtains were most necessary—the sun was so bright that in the afternoon you could barely see the letters on the computer screen—choosing the right fabric provoked in him the decorative equivalent of writer's block. Determined to find something strong enough to keep out the sun yet at the same time not dreary, he turned to Charlotte. At first linen or hemp seemed the best choice—but then there was always the risk that the curtains would look as if they'd been sewn from potato sacks. A second possibility (it went well with the sofa) was an old Braquenié pattern based on an Indonesian document and called "Toile des Indes"; unfortunately, in this case, he feared that the many mythological animals featured in the fabric might have "powers." Still another possibility (Charlotte was especially keen on this one) was to edge a plain cotton rep or muslin with bands of another fabric, perhaps a toile de jouy called "Le Singe et l'Autruche" ("The Monkey and the Ostrich"). And then there was the beautiful green batik that might or might not match the carpet, and the Bonaparte velvet, and of course the ever-present temptation (no matter what the house might think) of chintz, either from Colefax & Fowler or from Mrs. Monro. (The latter is the name of both a company and its founder.)

And what was the upshot of all this? Quite the expected one: More than two years after we moved into the house, there still aren't any curtains in David's study. Every afternoon the light pours in; David grumbles and Scotch-tapes an old blue bedsheet to the curtain rod. (For his own study, Mark eventually settled on a stripe in *or-celadon*.) Perhaps someday David will decide. In any case, we still read the magazines.

Cooked Water

THE CHALLENGE of writing about *acqua cotta*, the Maremma's signature disk, is the same as the challenge of cooking it: how to make something out of next to nothing. In recent years we have seen the gentrification of some of the poorest Tuscan foods, with the result that soups such as *pappa al pomodoro* and *ribollita*, once eaten only by farmers, fetch twenty dollars or more a bowl in New York restaurants. And *acqua cotta*—"cooked water"—is the poorest of them all.

According to Mauro the iron-fitter, at the heart of every *acqua cotta* is the phrase, *"Se c'era . . . "* If there was a carrot, you'd put it in. If you had a leek, you'd put it in. The essential ingredients are humble: onion, celery leaves, olive oil, and old bread, sometimes crumbled, sometimes in slices. (These are the only points upon which all recipes for *acqua cotta* agree.) To the soup, however, most cooks add a little tomato; they poach an egg for each bowl and sprinkle some grated pecorino on the bread. Fancier ingredients—spinach leaves or Swiss chard, a few porcini mushrooms, slices of sweet red peppers; basil, sage, parsley, garlic, *peperoncino*—are optional, as is using broth instead of water. Finally—but this is very rare; indeed, one might almost call it putting on airs—some cooks throw in a few pieces of sausage, too.

Despite occasional efforts at codification, *acqua cotta* remains, in Maremma, the subject of endless if good-hearted argument. Thus, in line at the butcher shop one morning, our request of the five women present for the *authentic* recipe led only to our being given five different recipes. (What they did agree on, however, was that the *acqua cotta* had to be made in a cast-iron pan.) Sauro's sister, the cook at the old folks' home, prepares a bizarre version that—because it is baked in a Teflon dish—resembles Thanksgiving dressing more than anything else. (You have to eat her *acqua cotta* with a fork.) The extremely refined version that Pina makes shows fidelity to the spirit rather than the letter of the soup, for she omits the onion and celery in favor of a nest of spinach laid delicately atop the broth and in turn surmounted by a perfectly poached egg or some fresh ricotta. According to Pina, *acqua cotta* is eaten all over Central Italy. In her authoritative collection of regional Italian recipes, on the other hand, Anna Gosetti della Salda firmly identifies Grosetto as the birthplace of *acqua cotta*. (At the same time, *her* recipe is basically one for mushroom soup. Ada Boni's version of *acqua cotta*—which she gives as one word, *acquacotta*—is one for bell pepper soup.)

In the end, like its Emilian cousin, the famed *ragù* or meat sauce that in Bologna is served over tagliatelle, *acqua cotta* exists more as an idea than a rigid recipe, as essential a piece of Maremman folklore as the *buttero*. And yet . . . *Se c'era* . . . How far we've come from Mauro's poor childhood, from those days when there wasn't enough flour, and pasta had to made from ground chestnuts!*

---

*Pina remembers that in her childhood, her mother would fill thimbles with chestnut flour and put them in the fireplace to make a kind of candy.

The Hershey Connection

URING our first months in Semproniano, we were often asked if we were German. This was understandable: Most of the foreigners who settle in this part of Italy are German. In reply, we would explain that we were Americans, at which point, inevitably, we would be asked if we came from . . . where? After a moment, we figured out that the town being named was Hershey, Pennsylvania, to which vast numbers of Sempronianini had emigrated early in the century. That neither of us had ever been to Hershey surprised some of the older residents of Semproniano, for whom Hershey *was* America. At first the Sempronianini had gone to work in the city's quarries; later they built the chocolate factory that would employ future generations of immigrants. Soon Hershey became known in Tuscany as the Perugia of America.

The Hershey connection endures to this day. Rosaria recalls that her grandmother, who worked at the chocolate factory, used to return every few years to Semproniano bearing umbrellas filled with chocolate kisses. Alfred Pellegrini (Rosaria's name is also

Pellegrini), the son of immigrants, now runs an Italian restaurant in a Victorian house just outside of Hershey. This year he led a tour to Semproniano in which the participants ate at a different restaurant every night and took cooking lessons at the same hotel where Pepe had run up such a bill. The tour concluded with a grand dinner at Pina's, which we witnessed from our usual table by the fireplace. It was a rather sad affair. The tour members seemed tired and eager to get home. As each course was brought to the table, Pina would describe it to Mr. Pellegrini, who would then translate, for although most of their parents and grand-parents came from Tuscany, few of the people at the table spoke Italian.

Then the *acqua cotta* arrived. Gazing at his bowl, Mr. Pellegrini entered into a reverie about his grandmother, who had become angry at him when he had written in his cookbook *(Recollections and Collections of Northern Italy: Her Recipes and Her Cuisine)* that he had always hated *acqua cotta;* the way his American-born mother made it, it was just "spinach water" with an egg in it. The memory of his grandmother must have touched Mr. Pellegrini deeply, for as he spoke his eyes grew moist. Pina, meanwhile, not realizing that his speech had long since moved beyond matters of gastronomy, kept interrupting to remind him that the spinach was organic.

Another incident stays with us. Although Giampaolo's father was the concertmaster of the Orchestra of RAI (Italian national radio and television) in Rome, his and Pina's own musical tastes run to jazz and sometimes reggae. After a couple of hours of Bud Powell, the people from Hershey started getting impatient. On their last night, they wanted to hear Italian music. "Dean Martin!" an older member of the group shouted hopefully, which led Giampaolo to pull out the olive crate in which he keeps his cassettes. With assistance from a few of the women, he sifted through them.

"Any Caruso?"

Giampaolo shook his head.

"'O Sole Mio'?"

"How about 'That's Amore'?"

No luck. "Who's Bob Marley?" one of the women asked, picking up a cassette.

"A rap singer," answered her friend, who was wearing a brown cloche.

Giampaolo continued to sift. Pollini playing the Chopin études, Victor de Sabata conducting the RAI Orchestra, Buddy Holly . . . To the great disappointment of the people from Hershey, and to Giampaolo's surprise, it turned out that he did not own a single tape of Italian songs.

In the end, some flamenco music for guitar had to suffice.

THAT same weekend—it was the beginning of porcini mushroom season—we went back to Pina's for Sunday lunch. At a nearby table sat four American men who, as it turned out, were also from Hershey, although not affiliated with the group from two nights before. After we helped them to translate the menu, we got to talking with them: They were on a tour of Italy in search of relatives. Only after lunch was over did we exchange names. "Scott Reese," one of them said, holding out his hand.

We paused. "I'm sorry—but Reese as in the peanut-butter cup?"

It turned out that his grandfather had invented it.

Later, we shared the story with various friends in Semproniano—Aldo and Gianni, Pina and Giampaolo—and were surprised at how little it impressed them. Although Aldo stocked M&M's and Kit Kat, Twix, and Mars bars, he had never heard of the peanut-butter cup. As we soon learned, despite their acute devotion to Nutella—that ubiquitous chocolate-and-hazelnut paste that most European children spread on their breakfast toast—most Italians disdain peanut butter on the grounds that it is bad for the liver. (Just as Americans are obsessed with their hearts, Italians worry endlessly about their livers.) Even more inconceivable to our friends was the idea of peanut butter as a sweet, to be combined with chocolate or, heaven forbid, jelly!

A few weeks later, when we returned from a trip to the States, we brought a tin of Reese's peanut-butter cups with us. "That guy who ate here, the one called Reese—this is what his grandfather invented," we told Pina, who eagerly grabbed one of the candies and devoured it. "Well?" we asked.

She smiled. *"Discreta . . . ma non mi stupisce."* (Not bad . . . but it doesn't stupefy me.)

We kept the rest for ourselves.

High Noon

WILLIAM SHARP, a Scottish poet who would later take the pen name of Fiona McLeod, traveled in Italy in the 1890s; in Tivoli he published a collection titled *Sospiri di Roma,* or *Sighs of Rome*—poems that sometimes "get" Italy as well as any ever have. "High Noon at Midsummer on the Campagna" captures the taciturn sadness of rural Italy and its people, as well as the fecundity of history. Although Sharp is not writing specifically about the Maremma, he represents well what it feels like to be here in the summer.

High noon,
And from the purple-veilèd hills
To where Rome lies in azure mist,
Scarce any breath of wind
Upon this vast and solitary waste,
These leagues of sunscorch'd grass
Where i' the dawn the scrambling goats maintain
A hardy feast,
And where, when the warm yellow moon-light floods
　　the flats,

Gaunt laggard sheep browse spectrally for hours
While not less gaunt and spectral shepherds stand
Brooding, or with hollow vacant eyes
Stare down the long perspectives of the dusk.
Now not a breath:
No sound;
No living thing,
Save where the beetle jars his crackling shards,
Or where the hoarse cicala fills
The heavy heated hour with palpitant whirr.
Yet hark!
Comes not a low deep whisper from the ground,
A sigh as though the immemorial past
Breathed here a long, slow, breath?
Hush'd nations sleep below; lost empires here
Are dust; and deeper still,
Dim shadowy peoples are the mould that warms
The roots of every flower that blooms and blows:
Even as we, too, bloom and fade,
Who are so fain
To be as the Night that dies not, but forever
Weaves her immortal web of starry fires;
To be as Time itself,
Time, whose vast holocausts
Lie here, deep buried from the ken of men,
Here, where no breath of wind
Ruffles the brooding heat,
The breathless blazing heat
Of noon.

Turkey Tetrazzini

O NCE a friend of ours sublet the Paris apartment of an American woman who had lived in France for many years. After taking him on a tour of the premises, she showed him the kitchen, which was stocked with all the classic staples of French cooking: *cornichons,* Dijon mustard, tarragon drying in bunches. Our friend was busy admiring these ingredients, deriving from their mere proximity all sorts of ideas about the refined culinary life of the expatriate, when he noticed the six boxes of Duncan Hines cake mix. "Eat anything you want," the woman said when she saw what he was looking at, "but touch my Duncan Hines cake mix and I'll kill you."

This story, which at the time we took to be about ingratitude and jingoism (how could anyone covet layer cake in the land of the *tarte tatin?*), is really about the stubborn longing for familiar things—even things at which, back home, one turned up one's nose—that with the passage of years becomes such a distinguishing feature of expatriate life. After all, though some people go abroad because they have to—this may have been the case with the woman in Paris—most of us who move to other countries do so because we want to. During David's twelfth summer, he and his mother discovered from a cooking show called *The Romagnolis' Table* that pasta could be served with a sauce that wasn't red. The recipe in question was for *spaghetti alla carbonara*, and the next evening, with a sense of adventure, they prepared some. Of course they had to approximate: instead of pancetta, a hunk of salt pork, Creamettes spaghetti, "Parmesan cheese" from a green cardboard shaker. The olive oil was a pallid yellow and hailed from Spain—or was it Greece? Even so, as they ate that first *carbonara*, it seemed to them for an instant that they could hear the Tiber flowing outside their kitchen window.

After that—years after that—we moved to Italy. When we first arrived, of course, we disdained anything that tasted too much of America, exulting instead in the Italian-ness of the things we found at the grocery store: peppery olive oil, nearly translucent slivers of Parma ham, wheels of pecorino cheese that the *salumiere* cut with a wire. Though rarities in America, in Italy such foods were ordinary; you could take them for granted.

In those early days every trip to the grocery store, especially a stroll down the pasta aisle, sent us into a rapture. We tried all the different brands of bottled water and studied the classics of Italian cooking—Ada Boni and Pellegrino Artusi—in the hope of learning how to make every dish we prepared rigorously authentic. Italian cooking, a poet friend had told us, requires above all obedience to the rules; we offered our obedience and as a result became proficient cooks. Soon we could make *ragù alla bolognese* the way the Bolognese do, and *arista di maiale* (roast pork stuffed with rosemary and whole cloves of garlic) the way the Tuscans do, and *spaghetti alla carbonara* the way the Romans do (as opposed to the way David's mother had had to). Soon wonderful food became something we felt we could count on (a very Italian attitude) . . . and then, one morning about three years later, we woke up wanting . . . peanut butter. So we went out and bought some (it was Dutch) and for a few days ate little else besides peanut-butter-and-jelly sandwiches.

In this way it began. Cereal was next—corn flakes, Rice Krispies, even Cocoa Puffs. Then cream of mushroom soup. Then bacon for BLTs. We questioned other Americans and discovered that they, too, often fell prey to culinary nostalgia. On visits home we lorded our superior knowledge of European cookery over our friends and families, even corrected their errors. ("No, you never put Parmesan cheese on mushrooms!") In Italy, we nearly wept over the absence of graham crackers, hoarded cans of cranberry sauce, even stole shamefacedly into the McDonald's on Piazza di Spagna to savor a Big Mac in an invisible corner, and invariably ran in to the director of the American Academy on the way out.

THE FINAL corruption was turkey tetrazzini, which is, despite its name, a decidedly un-Italian—one might even say *anti*-Italian—dish. (Chicken tetrazzini was invented by the chef of the Knickerbocker Hotel in New York to tempt the appetite of the Florentine soprano Luisa Tetrazzini, who was ailing.) Our desire for turkey tetrazzini led us beyond simple nostalgia and into a hunger for those dishes—lobster thermidor, steak Diane, baked Alaska—that in our youth had seemed to us the epitome of sophistication.

Memory, of course, was the real culprit. As Proust knew, flavor awakens the past, which is why the longing for certain foods so often encodes a more complex longing: for remote places, for childhood, even for the childhood longing for remote places. Longing for longing may seem like a snake eating its tail—and yet it was exactly the vague yearning for a Europe we had never seen that the flavor of Stouffer's turkey tetrazzini had called up in us when we were children, and that we now found ourselves wanting to recapture: that *World Book* daydream of some ur-Italian city in which gondolas sailed down a river lined with Tuscan *palazzi,* the Tower of Pisa bowed before the Bay of Naples, and the Coliseum winked in the sunny distance.

When you live abroad, the ordinary and the mysterious trade places. What from a distance seemed exotic, the very things in pursuit of which you left in the first place, lose their charm, while the alchemy of time and distance reveals in commonplace things—the things you took for granted—a surprising loveliness. This may be the secret joy and sorrow of expatriate life: By virtue of living in a foreign land, you throw not merely your history but your identity into relief. The past renders an unsuspected poetry. To prepare the foods of childhood becomes, in a very real sense, a brief trip home.

At the Terme

For some, social analysis is a bore. The longer one lives in Italy, the more it becomes an amusement. After all, the Italian adores holding forth, even on subjects about which he knows nothing. The man who runs the bar at the *terme*—whose name is Giotto Senzanonno (Grandfatherless)—was going on at length one afternoon about what he considered to be wrong with America. Only after America had been a democratic country as long as Italy had, he summed up grandly, could it become a country as great . . . well, as great as Italy. When at this point we felt obliged to point out that the United States had been a republic for almost a century and a half *more* than Italy—the latter having been unified only in 1861 (Rome wasn't included until 1870), and under a monarch until 1946—he was left at a loss for words. How both sheepish and vexed he was, that something so prosaic as a fact should stop the torrent of his eloquence!

The *terme* is a microcosm of Italy in all its gory splendor and piteousness. One cannot fail to observe that the imperative to make a "good impression" *(bella figura)* extends even to the swimming pool with its smell of sulfur. Here many of the old women wear heavy makeup and half a pound of gold jewelry as they bathe, lest any other woman should have cause to doubt that they have married advantageously. (The water is a litmus test of wealth: It will not tarnish gold but it will blacken silver.) Men tend to bring two or even three swimsuits with them, all whatever brand is *alla moda* that year. (Last year it was Sundek.) And of course where there is a man there is a woman, the latter, if not yet married to the former, already honing the possessiveness that will one day take the form, when she answers the telephone, of the question, "Who wants to speak to my husband?" or, later, "Who wants to speak to my son?" Oh, how difficult it must be to be a woman in Italy! Sons are valued more than daughters, and so the only way for a woman to make amends for the tragedy of her birth is to get married and have a boy. And yet life is rarely easy for these boys who have been breast-fed until they were five and pushed around in strollers until they were seven. One sees them, pampered and ill-tempered, at the *terme,* their mothers standing anxiously at poolside in case they start to drown, ready with a towel to dry them off when they come out of the water so that they will not take a chill (even if it is 95 degrees outside), determined to lead them to the john themselves and to wait outside the door for them just in case . . . in case of what? Is it any wonder that this country is so corrupt, when men are taught by their mothers that everything good in the world is theirs by rights?

THERE are two classes of visitors to the *terme:* those who stay at the big hotel and those who stay at one of the small hotels or country bed-and-breakfasts in the area. Guests of the big hotel must pass through an electronically controlled iron gate designed to look *importante,* but which takes half a minute to open and regularly malfunctions. (*Importante* is important to Italians. David once overheard a woman in a Roman linen shop describe a set of sheets to a prospective customer as *"importante."*) For the three hundred dollars or more that they spend per day, the hotel guests are able to use the pools two hours before day visitors arrive and two hours after they leave, and to reserve the best-placed *chaises longues;* only they may use the Finnish sauna, the tepidarium and frigidarium, and the recently-installed hydro-massage. The day visitors, by contrast, pay fifteen dollars to use the pools and an average of fifty dollars a night for their room.

We have the impression that most of the people who stay at the big hotel are not so much there for the thermal water as for the life of the hotel itself—one that looks back, after a fashion, to an earlier time. Thus they install themselves in the lounge before dinner to have a *tisane* designed to mitigate some particular complaint (poor circulation, flatulence, cellulite) or one of the yogurt or fruit drinks invented by Umberto, the bartender, who not so long ago won a prize in Evian for a fennel-and-strawberry cocktail. (The day visitors have a Campari and soda or a Negroni at a village bar.) Most of the hotel guests take their meals in the dining room rather than at a local restaurant. After dinner they go dancing in the bar, which has a disco ball, or attend one of the auctions at the hotel art gallery, at which paintings, furniture, jewelry, and *oggetti d'arte* are on the block. These are presided over by Renato, a bachelor who lives at the hotel, and his sister, who lives in town. (Several months ago the sister bought a small

dog—it was either a bichon frise or its Italian cousin, a *bolognese*—
and named him Marcel, which she pronounces "Marseille." Presently she started worrying that Marseille might escape, so she
and Renato took him outside and hit him so that he wouldn't do
it again.)

What the big hotel purveys above all is an illusion of good
health. In the mornings Kirk (pronounced *Keerk*), the only other
American in the area, and his colleague Rocco oversee aerobics
classes in which the participants go to great pains not to soil their
importante jogging suits *(tutti)*. The lifeguards smoke, as do most
of the guests, even while sunning by the pools. Painless and gain-
less massages are available.

The day visitors actually seem to appreciate the water and its
healing properties. They drink it from a small fountain with three
spigots. Once we even saw an artificial leg, complete with stocking and shoe, lying on the grass while its owner enjoyed the falls.
The day visitors have their own entrance, their own changing
rooms, and their own facilities, the men's with Turkish—that is,
squat—toilets. We feel pretty confident that the hotel resents
having to accommodate them, since they often arrive in large
groups and are greedy with the waterworks. Although there are
signs cautioning the bathers not to stay under the waterfalls for
more than five minutes, the day visitors regularly station themselves beneath them for twenty or thirty minutes at a time.
(What, after all, is a little hydrogen sulfide inhalation?) Whereas
the guests at the big hotel, finally, are often to be seen wearing
expensive official mud preparations purchased from the *centro
estetica,* the day visitors rub the blue-green scum that bubbles up

from the *terme* right onto their faces and have to be rebuked by the lifeguards.

For all this, the differences between the two groups are fewer than the similarities. At one o'clock, the pools and even the waterfalls are abandoned; the hotel dining room fills up, a long line forms at the bar, picnics (*panini* or slices of pizza from local markets) come out of baskets on the lawn. Money seems to be a significant point of both guest and visitor conversations; prices of houses and cars and clothes and toothpaste are discussed. More grown men than one might imagine stay in the children's pool because they are afraid of drowning, or think they are, since their mothers worried so much about them drowning when they were boys.

As for us—the pleasure of being, as Byron wrote, "among them but not one of them."

Piero

IERO, who gave us the potato roaster, was a retired gentleman who described his own humor as "corrosive." He dressed in dapper sweaters and trousers, was rarely without an ascot, and like Aschenbach in *Death in Venice* he rouged his cheeks. This was not because he was trying to attract the young but because his health was failing and he did not want anyone to know just how unwell he was. (It seems apt that by profession he was a restorer of antique clocks.) In the years just prior to his death, Piero, who had enjoyed a lengthy career as a Don Juan, served as cock to a brood of elderly hens: Aina, who with her sweeping muumuus, heavily painted eyebrows, and gravity-defying hair resembled more than anyone Agnes Moorehead when she was playing Endora on *Bewitched;* Sandra, who had been close to Wanda and Vladimir Horowitz and who expressed great perplexity when she learned that Wanda had left her money to "blind dogs" (presumably she meant Seeing Eye dogs); Giovanna, who had survived "one of those US Air crashes" and spoke obsessively of the hip replacement she had had to have as a consequence; and Gloria, who was fat, and whom Aina point-edly served smaller portions than she did her other guests at din-ner parties. Piero had infinite patience for these women, and they adored him—particularly after his second wife died.

Aina, like many women, professes to be above gossip, but she gave us an earful of it before asseverating, "Of course, I don't believe a word of it." This is what she said:

After finally obtaining a divorce from his first wife, with whom he had been on bad terms for many years, Piero moved to Poggio Capanne, a village near Saturnia, with his second wife, a German noblewoman named Beatrice. ("She was a lamb.") There they lived in what he described as "a kind of Eden." One evening at a party (Aina was also present) Beatrice and Piero had a squabble, after which, to get back at him, she flirted with some other men. He was furious and slept elsewhere. When he returned home the next morning, she was dead. The doctor said she had had a heart attack and fallen down the stairs. No autopsy was performed, however. In fact, she was buried with unseemly haste.

All the women in Piero's circle were obviously excited to their very marrow by the possibility that he might have murdered his wife in a fit of jealous passion, even if they insisted publicly that he could not possibly have been capable of such an act. And yet, Aina hinted, he *had* appeared to feel remorse as well as grief after Beatrice died, so one could not help but wonder if, after all . . .

"He gave me her clothes," she added. "You know Beatrice had a tiny figure. And they certainly wouldn't have been of any use to Gloria."

Da Pina

PINA'S restaurant is located in a former flour mill not far from Maria Pia's house. There are eight tables and a big fireplace that roars and crackles in winter, and over the fireplace a portrait of Artusi, author of *La Scienza in Cucina e l'Arte di mangiar bene* * and considered the father of Tuscan cookery.

The first time we ate at Il Mulino (this was in 1993), we were with an acquaintance from Salerno who was offended when Pina addressed him familiarly (that is, with *tu* rather than *Lei*) even though he had addressed her familiarly—but, then again, no one is more of a snob than a middle-class Southern Italian. As Americans, on the other hand, we welcomed such informality. After all, English has no distinction between formal and informal modes of address. Besides, as our late friend Lou Inturrisi once

*This superb book, originally published in 1891, has recently been issued in an English translation by Kyle M. Phillips III: *The Art of Eating Well*. In the photograph hanging over Pina's fireplace, Artusi sports long white muttonchop whiskers.

pointed out, the formal mode of address is quite often used ironically; the "ironic *Lei*," he called it.

With Pina and Giampaolo there was none of this: none of the mincing formality that Italians love. We all took to each other from the beginning, so that now they do not hesitate to tell us if we are putting on weight (or to congratulate us when we have taken it off). If on busy nights they have trouble finding a babysitter to take care of Martino, their ten-year-old son, and Margherita, their three-year-old daughter, the children have dinner at our table. (Margherita calls Mark *"amore mio."*) If we have been working hard in the garden in the cold months, Pina makes polenta with *ragù* and little rolls of veal filled with asparagus and mozzarella specially for us. When she serves her famous *medaglione di agnello* (more or less a "lamburger"), she makes linguine-thin French fries to go with it—also specially for us.

Pina is lean and sexy: Usually she wears miniskirts and silk stockings, a crisp white coat, and to finish off the ensemble a towering and equally crisp chef's hat. Except in August, and maybe also the end of July and the beginning of September, the restaurant is open only from lunch on Friday through dinner on Sunday. On Wednesdays she and Giampaolo drive all over the Maremma to find the best and freshest provisions—*marzoli,* a local truffle so called because it has its season in March *(marzo),* or vegetables from a secret market near the coast that operates like a speakeasy: If you know who to say has sent you, you are admitted to a room full of produce of incomparable savor— including such rarities, in Italy, as tomatillos, Chinese watermelons (their flesh is yellow instead of red), yellow tomatoes, and most amazingly of all, sweet white corn to be eaten on the cob. Not far from this place is a farm that sells nectarines with "white meat" *(carne bianca),* white eggplants that look like mozzarella cheeses, sheep's-milk yogurt flavored with lemon or apricot or wild berries, tiny and pungent fresh goat cheeses decorated with peppercorns or juniper berries, and aged pecorino.* Another farm, this one organic and run by Germans, sells a *passata di pomodoro* so flavorful you can eat it out of the bottle as tomato soup. In June these expeditions often conclude with lunch— spaghetti with chopped razor clams and wild fennel, then a sweet espresso—at a simple beachside restaurant on the Monte Argentario. (Pina is shrewd enough to keep a few secrets to herself, however. We still do not know where she gets her carrots, or her lemons, or her guinea fowls—oh, or her lamb.)

There is no written menu at Il Mulino. Instead Pina comes to the table and describes what she has on offer and never troubles to write anything down. Sometimes she actually brings out a tray of raw meat to show you how beautifully marbled it is, how perfectly aged. And what choice! Among the first courses (tailored to the season), does one want herb-laced *pappardelle* with a white rabbit *ragù* (the *ragù* is white, not the rabbit), or *bucatini* with a rich tomato sauce topped with a succulent hunk of lamb, the meat crumbling off the bone, or possibly gnocchi made with a

*Rosaria recalls that when she was a teenager, Signoria Idia used to serve chocolate ice cream made with sheep's milk at her *gelateria.* "So rich!" she says nostalgically. "Of course, you can't get it now. Pasteurization. Really, you haven't tasted ice cream until you've tasted it made with sheep's milk."

combination of potato and sweet beetroot and covered with a creamy pumpkin sauce, or plain potato gnocchi served with *guttus,* a local version of gorgonzola made with sheep's milk? Or what about spaghetti with March truffles, or plump *tortelli* filled with fresh ricotta and borage? And then there are the soups— *scottiglia* (a delicate broth of guinea fowl and pork poured over a subtle slice of olive-oil-drenched toast), or the hearty soup of chickpeas served with a small nest of the most exquisite *tagliolini* in the center of the bowl. (In Pina's view, soups are the glory of Italian cooking.) And then, after that, there are the *secondi* to consider . . .

For those of us who go to Pina's at least once a week, an added attraction is watching the other diners. One man, having worked in a Rome bank for thirty-three years and lost his wife (she developed a psychosis after giving birth to a stillborn child, was institutionalized, and after twenty-one years there committed suicide), found India, grew his hair long, moved to the Maremma, and now chants mantras between courses. A couple that owns a balsamic vinegar factory in Modena comes in periodically (hence Pina always has eighty- or hundred-year-old balsamic vinegar for her salads). Piero also ate at Il Mulino, usually alone.

There are often people there for the first time, too. The thing about Pina is this: One warms to her at once or not at all. Over the years we have learned to tell which of the newcomers will return and which will not. The ones who will not are those who find themselves at a loss for what to do in a place where they are not fussed over simply because they have deigned to bring their custom. (This was what our friend from Salerno wanted—to be courted.) And so they get up and down from their tables. They take restaurant guides from the top of the enormous wooden chest and read them through until the food arrives. They pace in front of the restaurant, where sometimes Martino plays with Margherita or rides his bicycle. We know that tomorrow night these people will eat at one of the more famous restaurants down the road in Saturnia or Montemerano, restaurants where they will be given a complimentary flute of cheap champagne, where there will be lots of water boys and waiters in bow ties, where they will be called *Lei*. And for them, this experience—an experience of dressing up and being made much of and paying a lot of money for elaborate and somewhat artificial-tasting dishes selected from a printed menu as long as their arm—is what going to a restaurant ought to be. Really, however, it is only an ego balm that emphasizes loneliness, a fear of connection. The great myth of Italians is their sociability.

Pina is an intimate experience, so much so that many Italians find her threatening. For us, after going to her restaurant, all seems right with the world. Both she and Giampaolo were orphaned when they were teenagers, which may be why they know how to make one feel that one belongs somewhere. Even their dog, Becky, is profoundly maternal, if in Giampaolo's words, a girl of easy virtue *("un po' mignotta")*. Once, when she had had an abortion, Becky was discovered in the piazza giving milk to a litter of orphaned kittens. Everyone gathered round. Tourists took pictures. Such a sight had never before been seen in Semproniano.

Sagra

For Americans, one of the pleasures of traveling in the Italian countryside is the likelihood that you will stumble upon a *sagra* or festival, usually dedicated to some particular food or dish. In our part of Tuscany, there are festivals celebrating, among other things, *acqua cotta,* wild boar, chestnuts, strawberries, pecorino cheese, *strozzapreti* (a fresh pasta made without eggs), snails, fava beans, artichokes, *bruschetta,* tripe, bread salad *(panzanella),* grapes, eel *(capitone),* and polenta. Another festival—this one celebrated each August in the tiny village of Rocchette di Fazio—features as its signature dish *penne alla Rocchettina,* the pasta served with a sauce of eggplant, zucchini, carrot, onion, hot pepper, tomato, and a little sausage. When we described the dish to Pina, she was unimpressed: For her, food that has no history is of little interest. "But it's *alla Rocchettina!*" we protested.

"You mean it was invented by a *Rocchettina,*" she corrected.

Pina's skepticism got to us. Make no mistake, much about the festival is delightful. You eat food prepared by local women off of paper plates while sitting at long tables and listening to old-fashioned music—all while surveying a view of hills amid medieval stone houses. And yet is it possible, after a while, not to notice that a layer of dust, stirred up by all the cars, has settled atop your plate of nonhistoric penne? Next to you sits a family—mother, father, two sons, and requisite grandmother in black—not exchanging so much as a word while they eat. Their silence inhibits. You worry that you may have ruptured the oil pan while trying to get the car down the hill into the impromptu parking lot, which was a pasture until yesterday.

Then there is the astonishingly bureaucratic system by which you pay. First you must wait in line for an interminable period while those ahead of you recite the menu to one another in theatrical voices and discuss what to have with an old man who takes down their orders with excruciating slowness and exactitude. Being an American, by the time your turn comes you have already long since decided on your order, but by now the dish you have selected—usually the one for which the festival is named—has run out. You make another choice. (Being an American, you already have a second choice, just in case.) The old man writes it down. You attempt to pay. You only have a hundred-thousand-lire bill. You wait for change to be found, or extracted from someone else in the line. You might even be instructed to come back to get your change before you leave. At last you are given the slip of paper with your order, which presently you hand to a young person in the guise of waiter. You sit down at the long table next to the silent family and wait again until the young person brings you your food.

And yet, and yet . . . (In Italy there is always an "and yet," a *quindi*, a *poi*, a *però*.) The table is shadowed from the August heat by the steep wall of the medieval church. The distant mountains are imperturbable, the valley set on its business, like a woman doing her shopping at the Thursday market in Semproniano.

That One I Don't Go To

SINCE coming to Semproniano more than a decade ago, Pina has made it her policy to cast her lot with those whom she perceives as the town's misfits. These include Luciano, who rides his bicycle in endless circles around the village and has a reputation for being not quite right *(matto)*. When we asked Pina about him, her answer was decisive: "*He's* right. It's Semproniano that's wrong."

Pina's assistant in the years when we first went to Il Mulino was a boy called Michele. He was fifteen then, very tall and skinny, with curly black hair; his sister, who looked just like him, was called Michela. (Our first Christmas in Italy, we had Christmas Eve dinner at Il Mulino. It was raining, and as Michele didn't have an umbrella, at the end of the evening he had to run home in order not to get drenched. How like a figure in a painting by Piero della Francesca he looked!) Then Michele went off to do his military service and was replaced by Maura. Maura—just a few years older—already had a tragic reputation in the area. Although her only means of transport was a Vespa, she nonetheless managed to cover a great deal of territory; Indeed, she had been sighted as far away as Grosseto, where she went sometimes to look at *ragazzi*. Yet her beau ideal was, and always had been, Michele.

Hers was a sad story. Her mother had died when Maura was very young, and now she lived with her old father—a "shit" *(stronzo)*, according to Pina—in a filthy and dilapidated *podere* not far from ours. The front garden was the final resting place of two broken front-loading washing machines, in which some of their chickens slept, and a still. A few years earlier, her older sister had decamped to Castel del Piano, forty-five minutes away, having first promised to come back for Maura—and, of course, she never did.

Giampaolo had once tactfully described Maura as having a "Renaissance beauty," which meant that her physique, to say the least, was formidable. To make matters worse, she possessed what he called a "great sexual fire" *(grande fuoco sessuale)*, and though he and Pina always counseled her to look for an older lover, a man in his thirties or forties who would appreciate a robust girl, she continued to have eyes only for young men such as Michele who would have nothing to do with her. Not so long ago she got a job cleaning the *caserma* (the barracks where the *carabinieri* live), which at first must have seemed like a dream come true: Here she hoped she might find true love. Ere long, however, she was disillusioned, for none of the *carabinieri* was any more interested in her than Michele was.

Michele, in the intervening years, completed his military service and came back to Semproniano. He had bought a car and put a Che Guevara sticker on the back of it, grown a beard and gotten a girlfriend. Though he was kinder to Maura than some of the other boys, he still didn't want to have much to do with her, preferring to hang out in the piazza with his friends when he wasn't working.

THE GENERAL refusal of Semproniano to accept Maura as one of its own, alas, is an illustration of the blunt intolerance that often underlies Italian life: a bigotry that has no role in our American fantasies and that explains in some measure the current hysteria here over immigration from Albania, Romania, and the ex-Yugoslavia. In a retelling of the Robinson Crusoe story, an old Jewish man is stranded on a desert island for twenty years. When at last the crew of an English ship rescues him, he takes the captain on a tour of the island, showing him the crops he has cultivated, the animals he has domesticated, the hut he has built, and so on. Finally he leads the captain to the middle of the island, where on two hills he has built two temples. "Forgive me, Sir, for my ignorance of your religion," the captain says, "but why *two* temples?" At which point the old man frowns and, pointing to the one on the left, says, "That one I don't go to."

This joke could easily be translated into a parable about life in Italy, where rivalries go back centuries and an unfortunate like Maura or Luciano, once branded persona non grata, has little chance of improving his or her standing. Thus Brunella has not walked into Carlucci's, or even spoken to Sirio, since the day eight years ago when she forgot her wallet and he refused to let her pay him the next morning. By the same token, Giampaolo has not stepped through the doors of the Bar Sport in more than a decade. When he and Pina had just opened their restaurant, he sent his brother into the bar to ask Miranda to recommend a place to eat. Even though she had never been to Il Mulino, her failure to mention it set Giampaolo against her, and he has boycotted the bar ever since.

"That one I don't go to" explains how it is that, in a town of fewer than six hundred citizens, there are two bars, two groceries, two bakers, two butchers, and two olive presses. It also explains why poor Maura always has a look of suffering and resignation in her eyes when she goes to the newsstand to read through the latest issue of *Grand Hotel*, or to buy her lottery card.

Our hope for Maura is that one day she will win 83 billion lire in the Superenalotto, buy a first-class ticket to New York, go shopping at Bergdorf Goodman, have a makeover, then return to Semproniano in a Chanel suit, driving a Jaguar. This has not so far happened, however, and so she continues to cover the province on her Vespa. Sometimes we pass her on the road, with her immense white helmet, her handlebars hung with plastic bags from Carlucci. Or from the thrown-open shutters of her house she'll wave and smile at us over the still. She has a gap between her front teeth, which in the Renaissance was said to connote lewdness in women. Our plan is to fix her up with Maurizio.

Snake Alert

O NE AFTERNOON in May—David had just woken from a nap, and was getting a glass of water—Tolo, who was in the yard, started barking with uncharacteristic persistence. David walked outside and found him in attack mode in front of the grate that covers the main gas pipe. Inside the niche an enormous snake sat (if "sit" is the right verb for what a snake does when it is not in transit), hissing with all its might.

"Oh my God," David muttered, in that eerily calm, toneless voice that terror elicits—which brought Mark to the window. Both of us are afraid of snakes, and as we had no idea whether this one was a *frustone*—a large but harmless species that eats mice and things of that sort—or a viper (although vipers here tend to be small and laconic, which this snake clearly was not) we went next door to fetch our neighbor Ilvo, whom long experience has taught which snakes are dangerous. "Aha," he said calmly when he saw the thing—still coiled, still hissing— *"Non è un frustone. È un aspide."*

Oh, great, we thought. Heretofore we had understood that the only snake in the Maremma besides *frustone* and vipers was the enormous *capovaccaio,* so called because it will wrap itself around the back leg of a cow and drink her milk, leaving her calf to starve. Here, however, was an asp—a hornèd asp. It was not the sort of thing you expected to encounter upon waking up from a nap.

After we had killed the snake—which was more than a meter long—by hitting it with the side of a pitchfork, Ilvo invited us to his house for a grappa. At the kitchen table he told us that once, many years ago, he had encountered a pregnant viper on his door-step. After he killed it, it burst open, and thirteen babies *(cucci-oli)* writhed out. According to Ilvo, baby vipers are so venomous that their mothers, in order to avoid being done in by their off-spring during labor, climb into the trees and drop them onto the ground. This is why you have to be sure to wear a hat when you take a walk in the woods in October.

Ilvo also warned us against ever cutting off the head of a snake: He knew of several people who had done this, and in each case the head had grown back larger.

ONE WINDY June afternoon when we were still living in Rome, we were walking through the Forum when, astonishingly, white myrtle flowers began raining upon us. Another afternoon in the Forum, during the winter, we had seen half of a small bronze-colored serpent twisting furiously upon the ground. There was something in both happenings that evoked Ovid's *Metamor-phoses:* Was the serpent from the union of the copulating snakes that transformed Tiresias into a woman? Were the myrtle flowers transformed lovers' tears?

Ilvo and Delia

ILVO AND his wife, Delia, have lived on the farm next to ours for most of their lives. During the Second World War, Ilvo left for a time: He fought in Sicily, where he met several Americans, then spent a couple of years in a British prisoner-of-war camp near Banbury. Otherwise they have stayed here. Every winter they kill a pig, which gives them enough meat not only to stock their freezer but to make prosciutto, sausages, *mazzafegato* (so called because it is so fatty that it will "kill the liver" of the person who eats it), and pancetta. Each spring they plant an enormous vegetable garden: carrots, potatoes, potently aromatic celery, onions, garlic, basil, parsley (which, according to Rosaria, women used to eat in large quantities when they wanted to abort), and peppers. Like Maurizio's mother, in the early spring Ilvo walks up and down the dirt road on which our houses are located looking for stalks of wild asparagus, pencil-thin and so delicate they barely need to be cooked. They have a taste almost like that of baby peas. Hunting for them is something of a rite: Driving along, we'll often see old couples, arm in arm, scanning the roadside, one carrying a basket in which to place the purple-green stalks, the other reaching with gloved hands into the underbrush. (March is also the month when the vipers emerge.) Sometimes Ilvo will give us a bunch of wild asparagus on his way home, and we'll make a carbonara using Delia's eggs, the asparagus, *grana padano* from Carlucci, and pancetta from Andrea. At moments like this it is hard to imagine living anywhere else.

Like many Italian men, Ilvo is very set in his ways about food. Thus every night for the past fifty years he has eaten only a bowl of broth for supper—even during the summer. And who could fault him? Delia's broth—made simply, with a hen she raised and killed herself, basil, parsley, onion, and that amazing celery, and perhaps served with a nest of her own *tagliolini*—is the best that either of us has ever tasted.

Their farm is a model of self-sufficiency. The sheep that Ilvo tends with his son, Fosco, produce enough manure to fertilize the olive trees, which give them plenty of oil, as well as the vegetable garden *(orto)* and the flower garden.* (Delia also prepares a delicious grappa flavored with coffee beans and the peel of mandarin oranges: It was this that we drank with Ilvo after killing the asp.) From the sheep's milk she makes pecorino and fresh ricotta; the surplus milk they sell. Just before Easter, a big truck drives down our road to their barn, where Ilvo awaits it along with a dozen trussed lambs, which the truck then carries away to the city. In their fields Fosco plants—depending on the season—hay, wheat, sunflowers, or *favette*, a feed for farm animals.

Only on Thursday—market day—do Delia and Ilvo go into

*Horse manure, however, is optimum.

Semproniano. The rest of the time, they depend for the staples they do not themselves produce on a brigade of traveling vendors who pass by once or twice a week. These include Rolando, the baker, his truck always stocked with fragrant loaves of bread, jam tarts, and marzipan cakes; the *Boutique del Pesce,* the side of which opens up to reveal all manner of fish and shellfish spread out on ice; a *salumiere* offering sausages, cheese, pasta, and dry goods; a tiny old man who sells potatoes out of the trunk of his car; a handsome youth who drives up once every two weeks from Naples with crates of oranges or artichokes; and lastly a Moroccan and his young son, whose van is filled with shoes.

Delia attends to the garden. She always knows exactly when—and how—to plant things: garlic in February, about ten centimeters under the ground; cauliflower at the end of summer; tomatoes in late spring. Roses bloom vividly under her aegis, as do gigantic hydrangeas, geraniums, even the tiny hot peppers that spill over the edges of the big clay planter near her front door at summer's end. Later she hangs them from the ceiling in bunches to dry.

Delia is never less than generous. When we go over to "borrow" some of her eggs (their shells are so frail that the merest pressure of a finger will break them), she never fails to invite us in for the inevitable glass of grappa or a slice of *crostata* warm from the oven. Usually we leave with more than we came for: not only three dozen eggs but several pounds of zucchini, a handful of parsley, and some tomatoes. Ilvo and Delia's house is typical of the residences in this area, in that it doesn't have a living room and consists instead of a highly ceremonial dining room (used only on special occasions), two bedrooms, a bathroom, and a big kitchen that is cool in the summer and warm in the winter, thanks to the wood-burning stove on which Delia does her cooking. And what cooking she does! One Wednesday morning, when we stroll over to talk to Fosco about the local elections and find her standing at the kitchen table rolling out dough for gnocchi, she invites us to lunch. We sit on simple chairs of pine and straw, the straw covered in plastic. Though it's hot out, Delia serves not only gnocchi with *ragù,* in big blue-and-white bowls, but grilled pork chops and slices of fried liver. Next comes a salad of cucumbers from her garden, which we compliment; before we leave she gives us about twenty: small and as serpentine as calligraphy, softer than their supermarket cousins, run through with a watery pulp of sweet seeds.

Although they have rarely been outside the Maremma, Delia and Ilvo are not unworldly. Their assessment of local politics is always subtle and acute; nor is there much in world politics that escapes their ken, thanks to the television news, which they watch assiduously and analyze trenchantly. When the wife of the Yugoslav president, Slobodan Milosevic, appeared on their kitchen television one morning (this was in the middle of the war in Kosovo), Delia turned to us and said, "I don't like that woman. She looks mad." As it happened, an editorial in the *Herald Tribune* had made the same diagnosis that very morning.

It is to them that we turn when something of a local nature perplexes us: for instance, the winged insects so tiny they can actually fit through the holes in our window screens. "What are they?" we ask. "How long will they last?"

"Oh, the little ones—*piccini piccini?* We call them *cugini.*"

"*Cugini?*" I repeat.

Delia smiles. "Now you see what the people here really think of their cousins," she says.

Frantoio

Trama di Maggio, olio per assagio.
Trama di Giugno, olio per lavarsi il grugno.

[Olive blooms in May, oil just to taste.
Olive blooms in June, oil to wash your face.]

O F THE many agricultural rituals that define the Maremman year—the cutting of the hay in May, the threshing of the wheat in July, the *vendemmia* in the autumn—none means more than the November pressing of the olives. Oil, after all, is the essential underpinning of Maremman life; unlike their cousins to the north, the people here almost never use butter—indeed, they barely know it, which no doubt contributes to their longevity. (Rosaria tells us that heart disease is virtually unknown here.) Nor does the making of the oil lack its element of pageantry. Indeed, when the young oil arrives, the people of Semproniano greet it with the sort of exuberance that the French save for Beaujolais Nouveau. To preserve its peppery kick, the new oil is never used for cooking but instead drizzled over a simple salad. Or it is drizzled as a final touch onto a bowl of chickpea soup. The most classic way to serve the new oil, however, is simply to pour some onto a piece of grilled unsalted bread that has been rubbed with garlic: This is the famed *bruschetta,* so often attempted and so rarely gotten right, even in Tuscany. For *bruschetta* must be a delicate dish, which is the point so many restaurateurs seem to miss. (The fact that the Florentine version is known as *fett'unta*—"greasy slice"—attests to its coarseness when compared with the Maremman one.)

For a long time Semproniano had one tourist attraction, the *olivone,* an immense olive tree more than two thousand years old. Before Podere Fiume was finished, we visited the *olivone* twice, sitting each time for a few moments under its capacious and maternal branches. We spoke of how, when we lived here, we would bring all our friends to see the *olivone.* Then in May of 1998—on American Mother's Day, in fact—an arsonist burned it to the ground. The town went into mourning. In particular the children, who had a tradition of walking to the *olivone* for a picnic on the last day of school, grieved the tree's passing. Ettore, Sauro's nine-year-old son, asked if he could borrow one of our computers to write an essay called "The Olivone, Burned and No More" *(L'Olivone ormai brusciato).* For months afterward, every time we ate at Il Mulino, Martino urged us to write a book about the *olivone.* (The assassin, alas, was never brought to justice, although his identity is known.)

In Italy, politics often matter on a local level far more deeply than they do nationally. Almost immediately after the *olivone* burned, dark rumors began to spread that one of the two political parties then vying for control of the town had been responsible. (The only thing we find hateful about the Italians is their willingness to destroy their own patrimony—the Uffizi in Florence, the Teatro la Fenice in Venice, the church of San Giovanni in Laterano in Rome—for the most selfish of motives.) As it happened, the mayor, who had won the previous election by one vote, was a member of the far right Alleanza Nazionale. One afternoon, to our great surprise, he knocked at our door and introduced himself. For about ten minutes he outlined his plans for the coming year—the new library to which he hoped we might donate some books, the new sports ground, the roads he was going to have paved (ours included). Afterward, rather delighted by his visit (there is always something grand about a mayor), we walked over to tell Delia and Ilvo that he had been by. They scowled. As we soon learned, they, like most of our friends here, were lifelong Communists, and were worried lest the mayor, with promises of paving, should lure us to his side.

To Delia and Ilvo, the burning of a two-thousand-year-old olive tree was an act not merely of vandalism but of murder. After all, in a town where oil is life, this great mother of a tree was looked to not only as a source of sustenance but as a force of good. When Pina offered us oil made from the fruit of the *olivone,* we accepted it with an almost mystic wonderment, not because the oil tasted any different from any other local oil but because it came from the *olivone,* which was born before Christ.

Today we try to console ourselves with the knowledge that each of our own trees, though mere striplings in comparison, has the potential to grow into an *olivone.* At the moment we have thirty-eight, which is just enough to produce a year's worth of oil for two hungry people and a dog. Being Tuscans now, we pick the fruit by hand just at the moment when the green has begun mottling into black (after November 2, All Soul's Day). This is why Tuscan olive oil is so justly famous; Umbrians and Apulians, by contrast, wait for the fruit to fall before they gather it, which makes for a more acidic oil. Then we pack the olives in plastic crates and haul them to one of the two *frantoii* in Semproniano (we, too, have had to choose), this one located in a warehouse behind the farmers' cooperative *(consorzio agrario)*. In the room through which you enter, tons of olives wait to be weighed and pressed, mountains of them, either in crates or in burlap bags through which a little moisture is already seeping. Usually there is a truck parked outside, bearing the immense harvest of one of the larger *aziende*, a thousand kilos beside which our five crates seem rather meager. Still, we give them to the *frantoiano* to weigh, and he tells us to how much oil we are entitled, using as the basis for his calculations an arcane formula that takes in not only the quantity of olives but their relative oiliness in comparison to other years—on average, about twenty percent of the weight of the fruit. We nod acceptance of his terms. Then he takes our olives and throws them onto the pile with all the others, for generally speaking only huge harvests are pressed individually; in the case of small ones, the olives of several different families are mixed together, which means that one can never say truthfully, "This oil is *mine*," though everyone says it anyway.

After we have deposited our olives, we follow the *frantoiano* into the next room, where the press itself is located. This consists of a huge tub and a stone grinding wheel, operated not by donkey, as in the last century, but by a sophisticated system of gears.

For sheer scale it is daunting. The wheel is easily twice the size of the *Bocca della Verità* in Rome. As for the tub: If you fell into it you would certainly be crushed in a matter of seconds. (One is reminded of Charlie Chaplin trying to negotiate the mammoth clockwork in *Modern Times*.) At the bottom a peaty sludge shifts and churns, while from the side a stainless steel pipe leads to a tap from which a stream of oil is always pouring. The oil is such a deep shade of green that you cannot see light through it unless you hold a bottle of it up to the sun. It gives off a compelling, slightly mulchy odor. This is the cold-pressed extra virgin oil for which Tuscany is celebrated. (Later, the pulp will be pressed a second time, producing a paler oil; later still, the crumbly residue—by now the texture and color of potting soil—will be forced, thanks to the addition of certain chemicals, to yield up yet a third grade of oil, almost colorless and used chiefly for deep frying.)

Now the *frantoiano* (we know him as Paolo, who in the summer works at the Bar Sport, and in the spring does construction at the *terme*) asks us if we want to take our oil now or wait until "our" olives are pressed. We think about it for a moment, then tell him that now would be fine, at which point he picks up the stainless steel container we've brought along and begins to fill it. As he does so, one of our neighbors, a farmer with a lot of land, walks in and greets us. Behind him we see his sons hauling in huge sacks of olives, and would feel intimidated by his bigger harvest (this is the curse of masculinity) were it not for the tiny old man who follows them. This old man is so clear-eyed, he has such a broad, winning smile, that instantly we want to know

him, to talk to him, to hear what *he* thinks about Slobodan Milosevic's wife. In his right hand he holds a straw basket containing
at most twenty olives, in his left a baby bottle—a *biberon.*

"*Buona sera.*"

"*Salve.*"

"*Buona sera.*" Jovially the old man greets our neighbor, Paolo,
us. (Like the *olivone,* he is indiscriminate in his beneficence.) And
who is he? An inmate at the local rest home *(casa di riposo),* tend-
ing for memory's sake a single potted tree? Perhaps. We don't
know. Instead we admire the aplomb with which he hands his
basket to Paolo, who weighs the olives before throwing them
onto the heap. In a few hours they will lose all identity, they will
be ground along with ours and a dozen other people's, pulp and
stone, into the great democracy of oil. The old man hands Paolo
his *biberon* to be filled: just a few drops, mind you, yet enough to
remind him of that green mother whose milk tastes like pepper,
and in whose vulnerable wake there now trails the acrid odor of
gasoline.

Shopping at the Hypermarket

I T HAS become our routine, whenever we drive back to Semproniano from Florence, to stop and buy groceries at the gigantic supermarket in Poggibonsi, just off the autostrada, between Florence and Siena. This supermarket is so big that is called an *ipermercato*—a "hypermarket."

In retrospect, it was probably a mistake to have gone to the hypermarket on the afternoon of Christmas Eve. After all, Italians have the habit of habit, and one of their most fundamental habits is glomming up *(ingombrarsi)*. When you go to the beach in August, you can scarcely see the sand for all the vacationers, whereas if you go to the beach in June, you will see only sand. Every family takes its winter quilts and coats to be cleaned the first week of May, thus crippling the dry-cleaning industry for a month. Finally, all those housewives who do not have jobs—women who, if they chose, could devote the entire month of December to the leisurely stocking up of supplies for the holiday season—seem to wait to do their Christmas grocery shopping until December 24.

No doubt, when we saw the line of traffic stretching from the parking lot of the hypermarket to the autostrada, we should have known better than to try to get in. That it was raining didn't help matters. Still, groceries are substantially cheaper here than at Carlucci, and this being 1999, we wanted to stock up on supplies in anticipation of Y2K calamities, chiefly bottled water and candles.* So we waited patiently, managed to find a parking space, managed even to find a grocery cart, and walked inside. Although the aisles of the hypermarket must stretch for at least a kilometer and are laid out to encourage one-way traffic, carts were crashing against one another like bumper cars as their drivers exchanged holiday greetings. Everyone was in a mood of simultaneous exultation and hysteria. At the meat department, women collected next to empty refrigerator bins, watching avidly while, behind plate-glass windows and using machines of impeccable sterility, butchers dressed like surgeons wrapped and priced an immense quantity of ground beef, necessary for Christmas *ragù,* for lasagne. In the vegetable department, on the other hand, lamentations could be heard due to the extraordinary fact that there was not a single stalk of celery to be had. (The truck carrying the Christmas celery was hours late, stuck in heavy traffic on the highway between Bologna and Florence.) This was a crisis of substance, as celery, along with onion and carrot, is one of the essential *odori* on which the Italian winter menu depends. Without celery, how can you make a broth? How can you make the *soffritto* that is the first step to any decent *ragù?* Meanwhile women in green uniforms unloaded bins of lettuce, chard,

*Older Italians feared the arrival of the year 2000 because it was a leap year, and according to an old proverb, leap years bring death: *Anno bisesto, anno funesto.*

chicory, spinach . . . but no celery. It would not have surprised us to learn that the shoppers had waited all afternoon, even until closing, for the celery to arrive.

At last, having completed our own shopping—though the water aisle was picked clean, we took the opportunity to lay in supplies of batteries and pasta—we steered our cart into one of the many long lines leading to the checkout counters. The wait gave us an opportunity to study the contents of other people's carts. One man was buying only lighter fluid and walnuts. Another appeared to be purchasing his entire Christmas dinner pre-prepared: two-for-one packages of factory-made tortellini, Knorr broth cubes, a veal roast already seasoned with garlic and rosemary and accompanied by peeled potatoes so that all you needed to do was to stick the tray in the oven; a far cry, this, from Semproniano. At the hypermarket, boil-in-bag risottos, long-conservation milk, and frozen basil are making inroads as well. This is a very different Italy from the one of which we had dreamed.

Haltingly, the line crept forward. A burst bag of flour occasioned one delay, an argument over a coupon another. Behind us we sensed a sort of wailing restlessness, heard metal clanging, babies screaming, voices rising with rage or affection or both. And not for the first time, we asked ourselves: Why did they all wait until the last minute? Well, because that was how things were done. And perhaps also (though this was a more mysterious concept to grasp) because the very things that were starting to drive us mad—the noise, the throng, the general sense of apoplexy—were the things in which they took pleasure and comfort. Perhaps this story is really about loneliness.

The Blue Hour

T HE NEXT to the last Christmas of the century was a quiet affair in our part of the world.

In Semproniano, the only public decorations were a modest tree in the piazza, elsewhere a few lights, a nativity scene. Brunella, who runs the frame shop, made a tree of gilded chicken wire covered with gold bows and white lights. One exquisitely blue morning we were in town at about ten o'clock, and as we were walking to the Bar Sport, a Christmas tree made of persimmons at the market collapsed. All the good citizens in the piazza at once fanned out to catch the fruits as they rolled hither and thither, collecting them in a basket. The next time we went to town, the persimmons—which here are eaten with ricotta and shavings of dark chocolate—were still in the basket, which had been festooned with red bows. A few of the shopkeepers gave a small present to their faithful clients. Aldo gave us a bottle of *spumante* and a package of marzipan cookies from Siena—cookies much better than the dry ones traditionally eaten in Tuscany at Christmas, which are called "bones of the dead" *(ossi dei morti).*

For two years in a row, we'd had lunch with Ilvo and Delia on Christmas Eve: a soup of chickpeas and fresh *tagliolini,* then fried salted cod *(baccalà).* The third year, however, we had lunch with them a few days before Christmas, and on this occasion David helped Delia in the kitchen since he was keen to learn how to make gnocchi. For a second course, there was baked chicken and rabbit; and then, as always, dessert, coffee, grappa, and easy talk.

On Christmas Day, the townspeople usually dress up and turn out in the piazza. Presents are not given to the children until King's Day, January 6 (though this is changing) so December 25 is a day for socializing and eating. For the first time in recent memory, however, Christmas morning was not cheerful: It was wet and sunless, and the only customers at the bar were old men who had no family. Rather than Christmas music, Stefano was playing techno.

Yet what made the morning most awkward, at least for Mark, were his pants. In honor of the day, he had chosen to wear a pair of red corduroys, toned down by an Irish fisherman's sweater. Still, they were too bright for the old men at the Bar Sport, who stared at them in disbelief. Mark remembered a story his father had told him many years earlier about a colleague who drove a Jaguar XKE and dressed similarly. When his Jaguar broke down on the highway, he went walking in search of a telephone. Presently he found one, in a biker bar. "Mitch," he told Mark's dad, "I'd have given a million dollars not to have been wearing yellow pants."

Later on the day got better. We had lunch at Pina's with our friends Paul and Pamela, a Canadian couple who, like us, so got

Italy into their veins that when they returned to Toronto after a few months here, they knew they had to come back. At Il Mulino, Giampaolo was wearing a red-and-white striped shirt and Margherita was wearing red shoes, so the red corduroys weren't out of place. (Neither was Tolo's red collar.)

Although on Christmas Eve Pina serves an all-fish menu, on Christmas proper there are no restrictions. We began with *fettuccine di pollo* (ribbons of chicken breast "cooked" by being soaked in lemon juice) and a salad of radicchio and apple. For the first course, there were Pina's classic *tagliatelle al ragù* (the pasta flavored with bitter chocolate) and *tortelli di baccalà* delicately dressed with clams and herbs; then capon stuffed with prunes and chestnuts. All the while, the fire roared in the fireplace, and Martino told us that *he* would take the order for dessert. He did, and we were served a nest of fried chestnut tagliatelle dusted with powdered sugar and pomegranate seeds.

Lunch lasted from one o'clock until five o'clock (the so-called blue hour here during the winter). Paul and Pamela returned to the house they were renting in Castel del Piano, we to Podere Fiume—all of us agreeing that the rest of the evening would have to be devoted to reading in front of a fire, after we had called our families on the other side of the ocean—a distance that seems greater on Christmas Day than it does the rest of the year.

‫‫‫‫‫‫‫‫‫‫‫‫‫‫‫‫‫‫‫‫‫‫‫

Immortality

‫‫‫‫‫‫‫‫‫‫‫‫‫‫‫‫‫‫‫‫‫‫‫

R ECENTLY Mark came upon some diary entries he had made in 1993, on our last trip to Italy before moving there:

Rome, 4/1

I feel terribly forlorn at this hour, the consequence of a surfeit of beauty and reflection—a line I perhaps ought to have written at the Piazza di Spagna, near the Keats-Shelley House. Antiquity is usually stern, particularly when seen against signs of the transitoriness of human life. To my left is the Pantheon; to my right a table bearing a silver tray laden with used espresso cups and sugar packets, a few grains from which have scattered and caught light. How exquisite this transitoriness is to me: Boys play catch with an orange; a violinist and an accordionist perform "Yesterday."

Florence, 4/3

This morning I went to the Brancacci Chapel in Santa Maria del Carmine to see the Masaccios—chiefly *The Expulsion from*

Paradise—again. Only Giotto rivals Masaccio in portraying ultimate anguish. I also went to Santo Spirito, which is my favorite church in Florence, for its geometry, its colors, its ceiling (like a garden of flowers), its simplicity, its lightness, and its absence of stained glass. It is a church that is intimate enough for a human being to have a relationship to it.

Florence, 4/7

David and I have made an obligatory visit to the Uffizi, where his favorite works are the Bronzino portraits in the Tribuna and Parmigianino's *Madonna with the long neck,* and mine is da Vinci's *Annunciation.* Yesterday, David took me to the Museo San Marco to see the Beato Angelicos, particularly *The Universal Judgment.* I have never seen art that so communicates a sense of wonder at the cosmos. For Beato Angelico, heaven is light and flowers and graceful motion. Beauty is *interesting,* whereas in Dante or Liszt the infernal is more interesting. For most Christian artists, heaven is an idea: Beato Angelico is the only one to make it tangible.

Venice, 4/9

I began reading Mary McCarthy's *The Stones of Florence* when I was in Florence and finished it on the train to Venice yesterday. (I have not yet begun her *Venice Observed.*) Her *Florence* is ill-tempered; most interesting, to me, when it is either anecdotal or interpretive—for example, when she discusses the drama of the figures of the four seasons on the Ponte Santa Trinità (Spring lost her head) or the sorcery of Leonardo's paintings.

I have never feared Florence, but I have been vaguely afraid of

Venice, of drowning. The first time I was in Venice was the night
before Ash Wednesday (the hours between midnight and dawn)
last year. Today (Good Friday) is the first time I am in Venice during the day. Venice, like the moon, has two sides—one light, airy,
transparent; the other dark, gloomy, tragic (as in Shakespeare's
Othello or Liszt's *La lugubre gondola*)—while Florence is a dark,
brilliant sun: so radiant that even its blackness, like a sunspot, is
invisible to the eye.

Venice, 4/10

I did read McCarthy's *Venice Observed* yesterday, finishing it
at midnight. She quotes Henry James, whom I am beginning to
like: "There is nothing left to discover or describe [in Venice],
and originality of attitude is utterly impossible." I wonder, then,
why she writes about it? As with her Florence book, the approach
is mostly historical, though sometimes she speaks more personally here—of her apartment, her neighbors, the goldfish. While
James is right that "there is nothing left to discover or describe"
in Venice itself, there are things to discover and describe in and
to oneself in Venice: the enchantment—in the original sense of
the word—of an *orchestrina* on the Piazza San Marco playing
"Vilja" from Lehar's *Merry Widow;* the bells in the campanile of
San Giorgio Maggiore that rang out at noon on Good Friday as
David and I stood under them; the cat that had lost its right eye
but still kept guard of a newsstand. Original or no, these are
among my experiences of Venice. And, after all, Venice is the city
of Saint Mark.

4/10, later

A final word about McCarthy: She writes that the two modern writers who have best caught the spirit of Florence are Aldo
Palazzeschi and Vasco Pratolini; of two sounds that *are* modern
Florence—"the clack-clack of a sewing machine and the tinkle of
a young girl practising on an old piano." This image of a young
girl practicing on an old piano tells me that McCarthy omitted a
third writer who caught the spirit of Florence: Forster. To me,
that young girl practicing on the old piano is Lucy Honeychurch
in *A Room with a View*. She, too, is part of the art of Florence, but
it is hard to hear her over the din of Vespas stinging the Tuscan
stillness; so unlike the bats, cutting silent, graceful arcs over the
Arno at dusk.

Venice, 4/11

Easter Sunday: pealing bells, Florian's, rain, an Easter different from every other. The Easters I remember are uniformly glum
and contrary, with the air of a foregone conclusion. There was
always an Easter cold snap that made the morning bright blue
but, by the time for egg hunts in the afternoon, had given way to
a nauseating heat—nauseating as the salty, sulfuric yolks of the
pastel spoils of the hunt. I feel at Easter the absence of mystery in
the diurnal. I am most moved by the penitential days of the litur-
gical year, by Ash Wednesday and Maundy Thursday, for these
are, to me, the womb—the wondrous nocturnal—from which
the spirit is born. This Easter, however—gray and wintry, passed
in a Venetian café-temple, a place of worldliness, and on infernal
Murano—has the force and generative power of night, rich soil,
death.

Florence, 4/18

David and I left Florence the morning of the fifteenth, based ourselves in Perugia, and visited Cortona, Assisi, Gubbio, Urbino, Orvieto, Montepulciano, and Pienza. I have been now to all the "little towns" Philip encourages Lilia to see in *Where Angels Fear to Tread,* as well as a few others. The physical world here during the spring is so ravishing, so shimmeringly beautiful, I was unable to experience it as fully as I longed to; oh, the sadness of the sublime. I began then to reimagine the heaven I have believed in: heaven as a sensuous condition, not as a place. Florence is "earthly" heaven to me because I experience it, and long for it, more fully than I do any other place.

THE HEART of these pages is Florence and God. Then, these were Mark's twin deities. (Forster was a third.) Now, if he has a god, it is a pagan god: an Etruscan god, or one to whom a temple at Paestum was built.

As for Florence: A deity it remains, but—like all deities—it is a troubling one. After living in the Italian countryside, Florence seems more "the city" than any other metropolitan place in the world; more than New York, more than Rome, more than Hong Kong. Paradoxically, it seems this way because it is made to the measure of man—one can walk there. (Contrary to what we imagined, one actually walks very little in the country.)

With time and understanding, the city called Florence has taken on a more ominous aspect than the one we attributed to Venice, for Florence is able to impel the body to its own destruction. One hopes to be equal to Florence (as if that were possible), but those who are not often commit suicide there: The city is an unofficial mecca for people intending to do themselves in. During the first days we actually lived there, a girl killed herself by jumping from Giotto's bell tower. The fall crushed her bones, yet her corpse shed not a drop of blood. Indeed, the only evidence of her jump was a section of scaffolding dented by her landing, and one of her tennis shoes, which had come off from the force of it. For half a century or so, Florence was also a preferred place of self-exile for English men and women whose homeland had rejected them. Osbert Sitwell, whose father bought a villa at Montegufoni, penned a remarkable poem about one Lord Henry Somerset, who, obliged by scandal to leave England, lived out his life in Florence. In the poem, titled "Milordo Inglese," he wrote,

> . . . *killing time*
> Is only the name for another of the multifarious ways
> By which Time kills us.

Life does not give up without a fight in Florence, though. Almost one fifth of what the world regards as its artistic treasures are found there, and the mere fact of their presence—let alone of their experiencing—impels one to live and to love, to build and to burn until one has given one's blood. (Oh, how potent a symbol of failure was that bloodless corpse on the scaffolding!) Stendhal's syndrome describes the intense and prostrating nature of Florence's genius (tourists collapsing before art), but it does not describe what the city makes one want to do.

No longer do we long for Florence more than any other place, although the love and fear the city inspires have not diminished in us. The longed-for place now is the country, which is rather like

Beato Angelico's place of light and flowers and graceful motion, but not only that. It also embraces an undying Fascism in which women with names like Adua (in honor of Italian victory in Ethiopia) and Benita (the feminine form of Benito—as in Mussolini) become furious if another Italian dares to speak even one word of a foreign language, as well as an undying Democracy in which there is no "we" set against "them," no *noi* set against *loro*. Every garden has its Lucifer, and it is well to lose the innocence that conceals the truth.

WE LIVE in Maremma not by chance, not by default, but because it feels like home. There is no doubt that life in a city keeps the majesty of nature at a distance: How comforting, in its way, is the local movie theater, or the Starbucks on the corner, or the newsstand with a thousand different magazines. Yet this comfort is ephemeral. The Mediterranean, though, is permanent. The sky is permanent. This multihued farmland, which has been cultivated for four thousand years and looks, after it has been plowed, like an ikat fabric, is permanent. Cypresses and umbrella pines are not permanent —not like the sea, the sky, the land—yet they live far longer than a man does.

Until a century and a half ago, almost all of humankind lived in the country. And *live* humankind did: laboring in fields, practicing trades (shoeing horses, forging iron, weaving fabric), lighting their houses with candles and fires and oil lamps, playing music, dancing, making love, sleeping—all the important things.

Living here is rather like being caught between the seventeenth and twenty-first centuries: Modern inventions make aspects of life easy, but remnants of ancient ways endure. There are village festivals celebrating the gathering of the hay and religious processions commemorating salvation from the Black Death in the fourteenth century. Ancient trades that the Industrial Revolution did much to destroy are practiced still. Gods and goddesses that antedate Christ are worshipped (though often obliquely). Here, at midnight on New Year's Eve, one burns branches of laurel to invoke the protection of benign deities in the coming year. Here, when one moves into a house, one waves branches of myrtle in each room to chase out evil spirits.

It was the playwright Congreve who wrote that man wants to be immortal even though he does not know what to do with the life he has. We live in a place that balances the past and the present, and that has taught us that all the rich seasons here are only a sojourn: This one, this one only, is the life we have, and this is the life we choose to live. Who wants to be immortal?

Incompletion

No house is ever really finished, or finished for long. The workmen leave, months pass, you cook and spill olive oil on the terra-cotta. Spiders build webs, you brush them away and perhaps leave a fingerprint. Candle wax melts onto the mantel. Soon you notice that the long drying of the plaster has left tiny fissures on its surface, that a little wine has stained the marble top of a table. Everywhere there are things you haven't done: One room lacks a bracket for keeping the shutter open; in another a hole still needs to be drilled for the hanging of a picture. Yet for all that the house is more beautiful, not less. In the words of Margaret Drabble, it has "weathered into identity."

When we were first restoring Podere Fiume, we resolved to buy a dryer, which is something of a rarity in Italy. (Italians—as generations of painters and photographers have happily recorded—prefer to dry their clothes out of doors.) For years, in Florence and then in Rome, we had missed having a dryer, especially on those afternoons when an unexpected rainstorm washed our sheets all over again. Then the dryer arrived, and though for a while we indulged in an orgy of drying, soon we found ourselves missing the smell of clothes that had dried under the Tuscan sun; we noticed that whenever we ran the machine, the lights in the house dimmed to about half their usual brightness. Presently we took to hanging things out again and used the dryer less and less. Now we barely use it at all.

We moved here to capture a dream less of Italy than of being foreigners in Italy, figures in a Forster novel. And yet Italy has a way of refusing to remain only a background. It grows into you, just as you grow into it. You begin to doubt dryers. After seven years, in ways we could never have predicted, we have become Italian.